To Henri.

Happy Birthday

Myra and James.

29 September 2011

— at The Chenière in Dover —

Chapter 8.

# BUSES
## YEARBOOK 2012
### Edited by STEWART J. BROWN

Ian Allan
PUBLISHING

# BUSES
## YEARBOOK 2012

First published 2011

ISBN 978 0 7110 3553 9

© Ian Allan Publishing Ltd 2011

Published by Ian Allan Publishing

an imprint of Ian Allan Publishing Ltd,
Hersham, Surrey, KT12 4RG.

Printed in England by Ian Allan Printing Ltd,
Hersham, Surrey, KT12 4RG.

Code: 1108/x

Visit the Ian Allan Publishing website at
www.ianallanpublishing.com

**Front cover:**
Nottingham City Transport acquired Pathfinder (Newark)
in 1997 and retains the fleetname for its 100 service from
Nottingham to Southwell. Here an Optare Versa, one of
five so branded, turns into King Street, its city terminus,
from Upper Parliament Street in January 2011.

**Back cover (upper):**
One of First Eastern Counties' Excel-branded Volvo B9TLs with
Wright Eclipse Gemini bodywork leaves the Market Gates bus
station for Kings Lynn, two-and-a-half hours distant.

**Back cover (lower):**
A Metroline Plaxton-bodied Volvo B7TL in Oxford Street.

**Previous page:**
Genuine company branding in London: a tendered service
operated by London & Country (which later lost its identity
to Arriva) with an East Lancs-bodied Volvo Citybus in 1991.

# Contents

# Once there was a way

In this tale of two cities **Peter Rowlands** considers the homing instinct, and how the buses in his life have summed it up.

*All photographs by the author*

Occasional houses start to break the monotony of the journey, then they become more dense, and finally the urban landscape asserts itself: terraced streets to the right and left, and ahead the beckoning mass of the city. And, up one of those side streets to the right, a tantalising glimpse through the car window of yellow: ineluctable proof that this is not just any city; it's home. Which for me, in my childhood incarnation, was Newcastle, though, to be strictly correct, this was actually Gateshead. The yellow flash was of a Newcastle Transport double-decker, skulking in the Low Fell suburbs at the most southerly point of its long cross-Tyne route. It radiated an extraordinarily powerful, almost visceral message.

It said we were safely back in the land of yellow buses. We made it.

I never photographed any of those buses at the time; the idea never once occurred to me. I did manage to take some pictures of a preserved example when it was running on a Silver Jubilee service in 1977, but it's not quite the same thing as getting a proper photograph of a vehicle operating in normal service, is it?

By then home for me was 300 miles south, in London, but it was around that time, on a fleeting visit to Newcastle, that I realised I'd better start taking bus pictures in earnest if I wanted to record the world I'd once known there.

London, of course, was a cornucopia of

*Left:* **Withdrawn seven years previously but running on a Silver Jubilee service in 1977, this Northern Coachbuilders-bodied AEC Regent III was photographed at the Tyne & Wear PTE's City depot, awaiting minor repairs. It remains in preservation and is seen regularly at rallies.**

*Right:* **In London in the 1970s there were still large numbers of Regent IIIs in regular service. This Metro-Cammell-bodied RT is seen in Edmonton in 1977.**

everything that had vanished from the bus world in my home city. Here I found AEC Regent IIIs galore (in the form of the surviving RTs), not to mention Routemasters, which still seemed comparatively new buses.

Contrast this with Newcastle, where the first Leyland Atlanteans were appearing as early as 1960. More or less all front-engined double-deckers had disappeared long before I finally left in the early 1970s to make my home in the South.

I realise now that, in amongst my many subsequent photographic forays to other parts of the country, my bus photography became in one sense a sort of two-pronged attempt to capture what I'd missed in my earlier life. In London it meant photographing RTs while they were still there and then Routemasters for many years after. In the beginning there were also RFs, Swifts, DMS Fleetlines and many other types that seemed new then but which now already seem like ancient history.

In Newcastle, during some of my subsequent infrequent visits, I found myself trying to re-create scenes remembered from childhood: Atlanteans roaring down Kenton Road in Gosforth, and yellow buses of any kind, glimpsed from the distance on the approach to the city environs.

Admittedly, the buses in Newcastle weren't quite right. Those from my childhood were little more than memories, so I had to make do with what was here now. But at least the yellow livery was relatively unchanged, and later AN68 Atlanteans looked as though they could be the offspring of the originals.

With the eyes of an émigré returned, I also found myself marvelling at sights I'd never

*Top:* **The Daimler Fleetline was London's idea of a modern double-decker in the 1970s. This one is seen in Farringdon Road in 1977.**

*Middle:* **The world turned upside down? A flat-fronted Bristol RE of United Automobile Services, incongruously painted in full PTE yellow livery in a gesture towards transport co-ordination and photo-graphed in 1981.**

*Bottom:* **A past imagined rather than remembered: an Alexander-bodied Scania of Busways on the Quayside in 1991. 'I spent little time here in my youth — it wasn't trendy then.'**

*Above and Below:* Riotously coloured local branding by Go-Ahead in the North East: a Leyland Olympian in Wear Express livery, and a Wright-bodied Dennis Dart with VFM ('Value For Money') branding.

envisaged when I lived there: Bristol REs and VRs in lined-out Newcastle yellow, for instance (painted that way in a short-lived burst of visible transport co-ordination by the PTE). Newcastle Transport had never operated Bristols at all in my childhood, and had withdrawn its last single-deckers in my earliest years.

There were parallels and contrasts. As the 1970s unfolded, London put into service hundreds of Daimler Fleetlines, while Newcastle (by now the Tyne & Wear PTE) stuck with its Atlanteans. Both operators experimented with Scania/MCW Metropolitans — eerily silent when new but bouncy for passengers and, over time, expensive for operators. Then London switched to the new duopoly of MCW Metrobuses and Leyland Titans and eventually to Olympians, while Tyne & Wear gravitated to Olympians as well but also retained an allegiance to Scania.

Perhaps more astounding to me was the variety of colours and identities that blossomed among other Newcastle operators after privatisation.

There was only one Go-Ahead Northern, but as the 1980s and '90s unfolded there seemed to be dozens of incarnations. To add to the variety, the PTE's post-1986 Busways company revived identities of businesses acquired years before by the PTE, and Northumbria's wonderfully bold livery added a further dimension.

London buses, of course, stayed predominantly red, but here too there was a sudden explosion of new colour schemes around 1990. In this case, however, the reason was route tendering, and the liveries really did denote different companies.

It was 15 years ago, around 1996, that it finally dawned on me there was no going back. That was when Stagecoach acquired Busways and soon started applying its corporate livery to the fleet. Goodbye yellow buses — and goodbye the illusion that home was still in the North. On several visits I tried to fill in gaps in my collection, grabbing pictures of yellow buses in a variety of familiar haunts, but of course it was a battle I couldn't win, and eventually I had to retire graciously and admit

*Below:* **Not the Gateshead & District remembered from the author's childhood, but at least the idea was revived effectively for a while by Go-Ahead in this impressive livery, seen on a Mk II Metrobus in 1996.**

defeat. Within a couple of years they had all gone.

London, however, still had its Routemasters — glorious, anachronistic echoes of an earlier era. And somehow, they seemed to insinuate themselves into more and more of my photographs. I'm not saying they reminded me of Newcastle; I'd always thought of Northern General's handful of Routemasters as curiosities from the South. But the London examples presented an apparently indelible link with the past. Until 2005. Then they too were gone. One day, it seemed, I was standing in Oxford Street, marvelling at their profusion. The next day, nothing.

So, is there life after yellow buses and Routemasters? Well, I have to say yes. I can't deny that Newcastle looks very smart these days, with its elegantly liveried Stagecoach buses (and I

never thought I'd hear myself saying that). But I think I've finally realised it's not really home. That's London — admittedly now without Routemasters (until the threatened replacement makes its appearance), but with associations — and enough pictures of them to last an eternity — and with an ever-changing mixture of more modern vehicles to orchestrate the life I chose.

Dare I admit it? The Optare-bodied batch of Alexander Dennis Enviros, stalwarts of the long route between Putney and North Cheam, are now my favourites — and possibly it's a combination destined to be as rare as the Northern Coachbuilders-bodied AEC Regents of my childhood.

Some things never change.

*Right:* One livery that set a standard of elegance in the North East of England in the 1990s was that of Northumbria Motor Services, created from part of United Automobile.

*Left:* A few hundred yards from his childhood home and 40 years on, the author took this picture of a Busways Alexander-bodied Leyland Atlantean in 1996.

*Above:* Newcastle in recent times: A Stage-coach Alexander Dennis Enviro400 at Grey's Monument in 2008.

*Below:* Present-day London and the author's new favourite bus: one of London General's unusual Alexander Dennis Enviro double-deckers with Optare bodywork.

*Above:* Genuine nostalgia in London in 1991: one of East London's RMC Routemaster coaches, refurbished for an express version of the route 15 into London from the Beckton.

*Below:* Still going strong in 1996 — a recently repainted Routemaster from the East London fleet passes John Lewis in Oxford Street. The route would continue to be Routemaster-operated for another eight years.

# Seaside Rendezvous

The streets of Great Yarmouth are host to a wide range of bus and coach types, particularly during the summer months, when the indigenous ranks are swollen by the season's visitors. **David Jukes** illustrates one week in August 2010.

Great Yarmouth's bus services have seen great change since the halcyon days of municipal and company ownership, when Great Yarmouth Transport and Eastern Counties enjoyed a virtual monopoly of services in and around the coastal resort.

In 1984 Eastern Counties' coach operations were transferred to Ambassador Travel, a newly created National Bus Company subsidiary; the new company was sold to its management during 1987 and ultimately was to base itself in Great Yarmouth. That same year saw Eastern Counties sold to its management — a status retained for seven years until sold in July 1994 to GRT Holdings, parent company of Grampian Regional Transport. Amalgamation of GRT and Badgerline as FirstBus (later FirstGroup) saw the fleet initially retain the GRT-style livery of cream with red and orange relief, which had replaced the earlier red with orange and cream stripes.

Great Yarmouth Transport, Norfolk's only municipal operator, marketed itself as Blue Buses during the post-deregulation era until its acquisition by First in 1996. The town's bus operations were then consolidated at the ex-municipal art-deco 1930 Caister Road garage, the former Eastern Counties premises in Wellington

*Below:* **A First Eastern Counties Plaxton President-bodied Volvo B7TL, new in dual-door form to CentreWest in 2003, heads south along Great Yarmouth's North Drive on 9 August 2010. Details for route 3 are shown on the piece of paper placed behind the offside front windscreen.**

*Above:* Route 3 was not monopolised by the ex-London Volvo B7TLs. Here a Northern Counties Palatine II-bodied Volvo Olympian, new to Bristol in 1998, is seen on Marine Parade. Again, the destination display is less than informative.

Road being sold for development. A number of Great Yarmouth-allocated vehicles originating with both operators received GRT-style cream with two-tone-blue relief, branded First Blue Bus, before this disappeared beneath corporate hues.

Outside competition had appeared in 1989 in the form of the Flying Banana town minibus services, which later passed to First. However, this era is not forgotten locally, as one of three Routemasters transferred within FirstGroup to operate the Great Yarmouth seafront and Cromer–Sheringham 'Coastmaster' services wears the distinctive Flying Banana livery of yellow and green.

A 2010 family holiday in the area revealed that First was still the town's dominant bus operator, the Eastern Counties company forming one half of the group's East England operation. Single-deck buses were a mix of step-entrance and low-floor types, either new to Eastern Counties or transferred into the fleet from all corners of

the First empire. A distinctive variation of First corporate colours was displayed by the fleet of Wright Gemini-bodied Volvo B9TL double-deckers branded for the long X1 'Excel' service linking Great Yarmouth with Lowestoft, Norwich, Kings Lynn and Peterborough. Former London double-deck buses operated on seafront service 3 linking the Seashore Holiday Centre and Hemsby Beach over a U-shaped route via the town centre. Sadly these were not the aforementioned Routemasters in heritage liveries (these, frustratingly, remaining within Caister Road garage) but Plaxton President-bodied Volvo B7TLs transferred from First London. So recent was their

11

*Left:* A First Eastern Counties Alexander Dash-bodied Dennis Dart, new in 1995 to Yorkshire Rider, is overlooked by the tower of St Nicholas' Church as it battles with the Temple Road traffic.

*Right:* This First Eastern Counties Plaxton Pointer-bodied Dennis Dart, new in 1995 to PMT, was the only bus to be spotted in service wearing this discontinued version of First's corporate livery. It is seen passing the Great Yarmouth Tide & Time Museum.

*Left:* One of First Eastern Counties' Excel-branded Volvo B9TLs with Wright Eclipse Gemini bodywork leaves the Market Gates bus station for Kings Lynn, two-and-a-half hours distant.

*Above:* The only one of First Eastern Counties' three-axle Olympians seen in service was this example, operating a Bernard Matthews contract. The 11.3m-long Alexander-bodied bus had been new to China Motor Bus in Hong Kong and operated for First PMT before moving to East Anglia.

*Above:* The sun didn't always shine during the author's Great Yarmouth holiday, as demonstrated by this photograph of a First Volvo B7TL on its way from Lowestoft to Peterborough on the Excel service. The end-to-end journey time is a shade over four-and-a-half hours.

transfer that most destination displays remained blank for lack of relevant route information. The recent recruits were augmented in small numbers by step-entrance double-deckers in the form of ex-Bristol and London Buslines Leyland Olympians, but only one of the fleet's ex-Hong Kong tri-axle Olympians was seen, operating a Bernard Matthews contract service, all the others being laid up at Caister Road pending disposal.

A number of other operators serve Great Yarmouth. Ambassador Travel remains in business and has diversified into bus operations, its mixed fleet evident on local routes emanating from

the town's Market Place bus station. In 2010 the distinctive blue-and-yellow-liveried Anglian Bus fleet of modern low-floor Scanias and Optares was much in evidence, operating to Norwich, Southwold and the company's Beccles home town, while longer-established Sanders of Holt operated its service 6 into Great Yarmouth from North Walsham, using its deep-yellow-liveried ex-Luton Airport low-floor DAF SB220s. Competition for First's service 3 between the Seashore Holiday Centre and the Pleasure Beach was provided by Cushing & Littlewood (trading as Our Hire), which used a Plaxton Beaver 2-bodied Mercedes-Benz

minibus on its Seafront Circular service. A further seafront service and guided tour was provided under the City Sightseeing banner by Awaydays of Wood Dalling, using a suitably branded open-top former London Transport MCW Metrobus. This ran at an hourly frequency for most of the day, its driver's statutory break accommodated by omitting one run at lunchtime.

Coaches were much in evidence, owing to Great Yarmouth's popularity as a holiday destination, its coach station alongside Nelson Road North being host to a number of visitors. The coach station was constructed in 1986 on the site of the Midland & Great Northern Joint Railway's Yarmouth Beach terminus. Most of the M&GN network had closed on 28 February 1959, including Yarmouth Beach station, which was converted for use as a coach station in 1962, although the majority of the railway buildings and platforms remained in situ for their new role until 1986. A pair of canopy supports and a short section of railway line are retained as a memorial to the site's former use.

*Above:* A 2004 Optare Solo of Ambassador Travel awaits custom in Regent Boulevard.

*Right:* An Anglian Bus Optare Tempo departs Market Gates bus station for Gorleston on a coast-bound A47 working.

*Above:* Sanders of Holt was operating this East Lancs Myllenium-bodied DAF SB220, new to Luton Airport. It is pictured exiting Market Gates bus station en route for North Walsham.

*Below:* Competition for First Eastern Counties between the Seashore Holiday Centre and the Pleasure Beach was provided by Cushing & Littlewood of Acle (trading as Our Hire, with 'Our Bus' fleetnames), using a Plaxton Beaver 2-bodied Mercedes Benz minibus, delivered new to the company in 2004, on its Seafront Circular service.

*Above:* The 'official' Great Yarmouth seafront service is operated by Awaydays of Wood Dalling under the City Sightseeing banner, using a route-branded MCW Metrobus that was new in 1981 to London Transport. The seafront service is incorporated within a guided tour of Great Yarmouth, which serves the Vauxhall and Seashore holiday camps in addition to the town's tourist attractions. Here the bus approaches Wellington Pier along Marine Parade.

*Below:* Ambassador Travel of Great Yarmouth was operating this 2009 Scania K340 with Caetano Levante body on the summer-season National Express service from London.

*Above:* Evening sunlight falls on the visiting fleet of touring coaches residing at Yarmouth Beach coach station. Those nearest the camera belong to Longstaff's of Morpeth, Dodds of Troon, Battersby's of Morecambe, Walden Travel of Saffron Walden and National Holidays.

*Right:* The art-deco frontage of the former Great Yarmouth Corporation garage sports three concrete reliefs, featuring a stage coach (the irony of a FirstGroup garage bearing one of these!), Stephenson's Rocket and a half-cab double-deck bus.

# Country buses

Rural buses are under threat as local authorities and central government cut back on funding. **John Young** illustrates country-bus services from around Britain, run by companies large and small.

The country bus has a long history. At deregulation in 1986 many feared that their lifeline services would disappear. Indeed, the traditional market-day bus service has all but disappeared, often due to a declining population and changed lifestyles. However, in many areas the network has been maintained or even improved, and several schemes have benefited from Rural Bus Grant or Kickstart funding.

Partnership working between bus operators and local authorities linked to effective marketing and targeted investment has resulted in significant growth in patronage. The expansion of Western Greyhound in Cornwall and the InterConnect network in Lincolnshire are well-known examples, but there are many others.

More recently new challenges have presented themselves. Cost pressures are a growing issue as bus operators have to contend with increased fuel prices, a reduction in Bus Service Operators Grant (fuel duty rebate) and reduced concessionary fare scheme settlements, and local authorities have had their budgets reduced under the Government's 2010 Comprehensive Spending Review.

Some villages enjoy a reasonable level of service simply because they are on a line of route between key traffic objectives. As green issues climb the agenda, there is evidence that in some areas people are prepared to try the bus for some of their journeys. In other areas the presence of tourists through the season is a welcome boost and helps to maintain the viability of country routes.

This collection of recent views is a celebration of the country bus in the 21st century.

*Below:* Express Motors' network of services in Gwynedd expanded at the end of 2010 with the takeover of routes operated formerly by Silver Star. Its modern fleet includes two MAN 18.220s with rare Marcopolo bodywork, one of which is seen leaving the Oakeley Arms interchange point at Tan-y-Bwlch on a journey from Porthmadog to Blaenau Ffestiniog.

*Right:* Padarn Bus has expanded through acquisition of the KMP business and by winning tendered services. A former Bullock's of Cheadle Leyland Olympian/ East Lancs climbs the Llanberis Pass on service S1, part of the long-established Snowdon Sherpa network.

*Left:* A Ford Transit of RH Transport Services waits time in attractive Woodstock before working the 203 service to Kidlington. This service offers four trips a day, running Monday to Friday only, and following retendering is now provided by Heyfordian.

*Right:* Stagecoach in Lincolnshire, in partnership with the county council, is involved in a number of InterConnect-branded services, on which effective marketing has resulted in a growth in patronage, leading to further investment. Here a Volvo B7TL/East Lancs Vyking pauses at Welton Green on a journey from Grimsby to Lincoln.

*Right:* Having just passed under the Manchester–Sheffield railway line, an ex-Trent MAN/Optare Vecta operated by Hulleys of Baslow enters Hathersage en route from Yorkshire Bridge Inn and Bamford. Other journeys on this infrequent service are provided by Wellglade subsidiary TM Travel.

*Left:* An ex-Dennis's Dennis Dart SLF/ Plaxton Pointer of Stagecoach Manchester sets off from the rural terminus of service 191 at Middlewood to return to the more urban environs of the A6 and Stockport. The tender for this service has since passed to Bakerbus, which operates it as the 391.

*Right:* Trent Barton service 199 (Buxton– Stockport–Manchester Airport) covers the whole spectrum of bus operation, from narrow lanes to motorway running. On a cold day in February 2010 a Scania L94UB/ Wright Solar passes Batham Gate, on the Peak Dale deviation made by some journeys,

*Right:* Centrebus assumed operation of trans-Pennine service 528 (Halifax–Rochdale via Ripponden) from First West Yorkshire in January 2010. It uses four Optare Tempos, one of which is seen at Lydgate. The service operates on an hourly frequency, including evenings, seven days a week.

*Left:* First West Yorkshire operates a network of services, branded as Holmfirth Connect, which provide a number of village links, including the 313 to Hepworth via Scholes. Double-deckers are routinely used, as evidenced by this view of a Volvo Olympian/ Alexander Royale passing a splendid hardware shop in Holmfirth.

*Right:* Pecket Well is a small village which benefits from Keighley & District's service 500 from Keighley to Hebden Bridge via Haworth and Oxenhope Moor. An hourly service is provided during daytime hours, Sundays included. Here a Volvo B7RLE/Wright Eclipse generates no additional custom as it passes through on a Sunday working.

*Right:* Tyrer Bus provides a number of services in Lancashire and West Yorkshire. The vast majority are supported by local-authority funding, among them the P70 (Clitheroe–Nelson), operated by an Optare Solo. It is pictured in the idyllic setting of Downham, an attractive village, at the foot of Pendle Hill, devoid of road markings, cables, TV aerials and satellite dishes.

*Left:* Pennine Motors is a very traditional operation with the majority of its network in North Yorkshire — not the most promising bus-operating territory. The fleet is predominantly made up of Dennis Darts. An unusual Wright-bodied example is seen passing through Settle en route from Giggleswick to Skipton, hub of the company's operations. Low-floor buses did not arrive in the fleet until 2010.

*Right:* Pride of the Dales operates a small network of services based on Grassington, where one of its Optare Solos is seen in the cobbled square on a journey to Buckden. These services were once the responsibility of West Yorkshire Road Car Co, which maintained a small depot in the town.

*Right:* York Pullman is involved in the long-established and popular Dalesbus network. Whilst changes and reductions have been implemented in recent times, many travel opportunities remain available, even on Sundays in winter. This ex-Translink Leyland Tiger/Alexander (Belfast) N-type has arrived at journey's end of 'Yorkshire Dalesman' service 800, being seen parked alongside the old railway station at Hawes.

*Right:* Stagecoach in Cumbria operates a number of scenic routes serving the Lake District. Among these is the 108, which runs alongside Ullswater on its journey from Penrith to Patterdale, where a former Manchester Volvo B10M/Alexander PS, by now in the twilight of its career, is pictured waiting time at the terminus. On schooldays most journeys are worked by a Volvo Olympian, to cater for school loading requirements.

On Lakes services 77/77a, which traverse the challenging Honister Pass, Stagecoach in Cumbria uses two Optare Solo SlimLines. Here one squeezes through Grange-in-Borrowdale on its first day of operation in March 2010.

*Left:* A DAF SB3000/ Plaxton Prima of Arriva North East calls at Craster harbour on a northbound 501 journey from Newcastle to Belford, where an onward connection to Berwick will be provided by service 505. The full journey takes three and a quarter hours.

*Right:* Stagecoach in the Highlands has responsibility for service 919, which links Inverness with Fort William. This forms part of the Scottish Citylink network, so the appearance of a Stagecoach-liveried Volvo B10M/Plaxton Premiere, pictured having just crossed the Caledonian Canal as it leaves Fort Augustus, was unusual.

*Left:* Shiel Buses, based in the remote Argyll village of Acharacle, is responsible for the Mallaig town service, grandly numbered 500 and worked by this long-wheelbase Optare Solo. In the background can be seen the Caledonian MacBrayne ferry *MV Coruisk.*

# Displaying your wares

**Gavin Booth** takes a look at advertising in the days when bus manufacturers were competing for a multitude of orders.

*All images from the author's collection*

Pick up one of today's bus-industry trade magazines and look for adverts for new buses and coaches, and you'll be lucky if you find any. Sure, there are pages of ads for used buses that you can buy or lease, but manufacturers seem reluctant to spend money to promote their products. Is it because they are careful with their money? Probably so. Is it because they recognise that there is considerably less choice than there used to be, so they assume that anyone wanting to buy a new vehicle knows where to go? Almost certainly. And could it be that it is because the vast majority of new vehicles are bought by a reducing number of customers that can be reached more effectively by personal contact? Of course.

It was not always thus. Back in the 1950s, when the British bus industry was working hard to recover from the restrictions of six years of war and another five years of austerity, there were manufacturers virtually falling over each other to trumpet their products and convince a much wider selection of potential customers that placing an order would solve all their problems.

Today if you are a bus builder you have to court the people at the mega-groups who hold the corporate purse and who are often in a strong position to negotiate very advantageous prices for the bulk orders they place. Fifty-plus years ago you had London Transport, big municipal fleets like Birmingham, Glasgow, Leeds, Liverpool, Manchester and Sheffield, Scottish Bus Group and the BET-group companies — all buying substantial numbers of new buses. Although BET and SBG would place bulk orders for their operating companies, there was some scope for negotiation and preferences for certain chassis or body builders could be accommodated. The buses of the other big group, Tilling, were supplied by the in-house builders, Bristol and Eastern Coach Works, so there was no real scope to break this supply monopoly.

And while today you can reckon that there are fewer than 10 chassis or complete-vehicle builders supplying most of the needs of the UK bus market (and just slightly more catering for coach operators) back in 1950 there were more than 30 chassis and body builders competing for business, all of them UK-based — unlike the current situation, where only Alexander Dennis, Optare, Plaxton and Wrightbus products are actually built in the UK. The January 1950 issue of the monthly *Bus & Coach* had 88 pages of advertisements to 40 pages of editorial; by February 1960 the advertisement pages were down to 50, while the editorial pages were still at 40.

So why were there so many builders fighting for business in 1950? Firstly, the industry had grown through the 1930s, and most of the biggest players were well established, usually building both buses and trucks and in many cases developing their own engines and gearboxes for their own chassis. Then there were the newcomers which recognised that there would be a huge demand for new buses to replace the time-expired buses that would themselves have been replaced but for the war.

There was a bewildering selection of bus and coach bodybuilders too. Again, some were the big names that were able to handle the major orders, but there were many more small builders that had grown up in the early-postwar years and which could turn their hand to everything from refurbishment — and there was a big appetite for this to keep the wheels turning — to rebodying and new bodies on new chassis. Bus builders were directed to concentrate on export markets to rebuild the UK economy, so home-market customers often found they had to wait for some years to take delivery of buses from their chosen suppliers. The solution was to turn to suppliers that they would never normally patronise, which could supply small batches of new buses or offer a rebuilding or rebodying service.

Some advertisers went for a simple message — a logo, an address and a photograph of a recent delivery, with virtually no other copy. Others boasted about recent orders. Some of the smaller coachbuilders showed commendable optimism by

*Left:* Welsh Metal Industries was one of the smaller bodybuilders that emerged in the early-postwar years. It used aluminium and 'aircraft principles' — something that builders had learned from the wartime years. The advert shows Caerphilly Castle — WMI was based in the town — and a Foden double-decker for the independent operator, West Wales. Foden was one of the chassis builders that dabbled in the bus market in the postwar years but decided to concentrate on trucks instead.

talking out full-page adverts. And you got the impression that someone at Leyland was obsessed by figures. Leyland threw acres of statistics at readers of its adverts in the trade monthlies. In 1953 it quoted fuel-consumption figures for its new lightweight Tiger Cub single-decker, ranging from 9.95 to an impressive 16.5mpg, though it may have slightly shot itself in the foot by pointing out that 13.57mpg was '3mpg better than Royal Tigers on the same route'. Later the same year it was showing how little time it took to remove and re-fit major units on the Tiger Cub chassis. In 1956 it was boasting how 'two out of every three double-deckers operating in Great Britain are TITANS [its capitals, and its italics to follow] … or *twice as many as all other makers combined!*'

As the cost of fuel rose and the need to economise became essential, weight-saving was

a dominant feature in much 1950s advertising. In 1953 Willowbrook was promoting the 'Willowbrook-Brush' light-alloy body, which contributed just 1 ton 10cwt to a single-deck bus weighing 5 tons 8cwt. The same year Harrington promoted a complete chassisless coach weighing 4 tons 15cwt. In 1954 Burlingham was telling readers how its new lightweight Seagull coach body weighed just 2 tons 8cwt, and the following year Windover was advertising its new lightweight body (2 tons 4cwt of a complete coach weighing 5 tons 12cwt). Guy's new Warrior chassis (3 tons 8cwt) was being sold as 'the cheapest and the lightest high-class underfloor[-engined] chassis' when it appeared in 1956, and in 1957 Albion launched its Aberdonian with an unladen

**SAUNDERS—ROE**
(ANGLESEY) LTD.
**ALL METAL BODYWORK**

RIBBLE specify SARO bodies for their 50 new Tiger Cub chassis

*Right:* Saunders-Roe blossomed briefly in the postwar years, clocking up some impressive export sales, bodying London Transport RTs and developing the widely admired Saro body, as featured in this distinctive 1953 advert, making good use of the two colours that were available to the advertiser. The BET group bought the Saro body on Leyland Tiger Cub; this Ribble example trumpets the 50-bus order it had received from that company.

*Right:* AEC started the 1950s in a strong position, vying with Leyland to be the UK's market leader in terms of bus sales. It was supplying its Regent chassis in substantial numbers to London Transport and it was winning healthy orders for its Regal and Regent from UK and export customers. The mid-engined Regal IV was introduced in 1949 but operators were clamouring for lighter-weight buses and AEC's response was the Reliance, as featured in this advert that appeared in 1954, the year after the Reliance was introduced. In this rural scene a Roe-bodied Reliance coach passes hikers as it powers up a hill.

*Left:* Although the Regent was its staple double-deck chassis for many years, the ACV group, which included AEC and Park Royal, developed the Bridgemaster as a low-height model in the Bristol Lodekka mould. This advert appeared at the time the Bridgemaster was launched, in 1956, and uses an artist's impression of the new bus; colour photos were rarely used in bus adverts at the time. The Bridgemaster was not a great success. AEC 'merged' with arch-rival Leyland in 1962.

weight of less than 5 tons and fuel consumption of more than 20mpg.

So there was everything to play for, and smaller bodybuilders and some of the less common chassis builders found themselves winning orders from the most unexpected sources. As we now know, this situation would not last, and gradually the major bus builders got their act together with new models, and the smaller builders fell by the wayside. But the adverts that appeared in the trade magazines in the 1950s give us an idea of just how keen bus builders large and small were to ensure that their name and their products stayed firmly before the people who made the buying decisions. And of course it wasn't just the vehicles. These magazines include adverts for literally every part of a bus that could be supplied as original equipment, or equipment for operators to keep their buses on the road.

But for this piece we're sticking with the buses and coaches, and a quick look at how they were advertised in the 1950s, with some comments on the manufacturers and their products.

*Below:* Leyland's first underfloor-engined type was the Olympic, an integral bus developed with MCW. This 1950 advert features a 27ft 6in-long version, but underfloor-engined chassis really took off just as 30ft-long single-deckers were legalised. The Olympic went on to be a successful export model while UK operators confirmed their preference for separate chassis and bodies. Note that both this and the Sentinel advert use just two colours, with black-and-white photos — with colour added in the case of the Olympic. Ribble also sampled the Olympic after its flirtation with Sentinel but reverted to Leyland chassis.

*Above:* Sentinel, a long-established company that had little experience in the bus market stole a march on the big players when it introduced its integral underfloor-engined STC4 model in 1948, and managed to sell six of the 27ft 6in-long bus and 14 of the 30ft STC6 model to long-standing Leyland fan Ribble, as featured in this 1951 advert. Although Sentinel enjoyed brief success, AEC and Leyland soon caught up with underfloor-engined models.

MORE POWER ...
MORE ECONOMY...
FULL LUXURY

Leyland 'TIGER-CUB' COACH

- LUXURY SEATING AND AMPLE LUGGAGE SPACE FOR 41 PASSENGERS
- 108 h.p. UNDERFLOOR DIESEL ENGINE WITH GREATER FUEL ECONOMY
- AIR BRAKES STANDARDISED

The 'Tiger Cub' is now available as a coach for the 1954 coaching season! Fitted with a more powerful engine than the 'Tiger Cub' bus, it develops 108 h.p. and provides an even greater power-weight ratio, greater economy, and, withal, a lively performance. This added engine power enables the Company to offer a coach for a gross laden weight of 9 tons 10 cwt., a figure which allows for 41 passengers seated in luxury, and with ample luggage.

LEYLAND MOTORS LTD
Head Office & Works: LEYLAND · LANCS · ENGLAND
London Office & Export Division: HANOVER HOUSE · HANOVER SQUARE
LONDON, W.1.

*Left:* Leyland and AEC quickly responded to calls from operators for lighter-weight single-deck chassis. Leyland's was the Tiger Cub, here in a 1954 advert for the newly introduced coach version. It carries an Alexander body, as did many early Tiger Cub coaches, in colours inappropriate to the Western SMT company — which never bought any.

*Right:* Leyland's model range typically mirrored AEC's, although in the mid-1950s Leyland opted for a far more revolutionary approach to double-deck design than AEC's contemporary Bridgemaster. The Atlantean, introduced in 1956 when this advert appeared, was a rear-engined low-height integral model, paving the way for what would become the standard layout for double-deckers for the next 40 years. Although the copy in Leyland's advert suggests that the Atlantean reflected operators' ideas, in fact these same operators made it very clear that an integral bus like this was not what they wanted. They were looking for a chassis that could be bodied by their favoured suppliers, and Leyland rushed back to the drawing-board to produce an Atlantean chassis two years later.

The bus with your ideas
... but built by us

The 'Atlantean' is our interpretation of your ideas on modern bus design. Its reception at the Commercial Vehicle Show was highly gratifying to us ... and, we hope, to those whose forward-thinking ideals were our inspiration. Almost without exception, operators praised the driver-controlled enclosed front entrance and the way it simplified fare collection. The 'Atlantean's' earning capacity with 78 seats, and its ability to operate when lightly loaded at no greater cost than a conventional bus appealed with especial force to those with peak load problems. They gave us bouquets for the built-in heating and ventilating system, on the engine accessibility and on the thought devoted to simplified control and driver's comfort. They gave us full marks for the remarkable manoeuvrability of the 'Atlantean' (equal to that of the ordinary 27-foot double-decker) and its low overall height enabling it to negotiate low bridges.

All in all, the general consensus of opinion supported the view of the trade press that the 'Atlantean' "initiated a major trend in double-deck layout".

Leyland
78 seater
'ATLANTEAN'

LEYLAND MOTORS LTD. · LEYLAND · LANCS · ENGLAND
Sales Division: HANOVER HOUSE · HANOVER SQUARE · LONDON, W.1.

**EARLY DELIVERY of single-deck chassis for 36–40 SEAT COACHES**

## Daimler . . . basis of a fine coach

Arrangements with a number of leading coachbuilders make possible the quick delivery of complete vehicles.

*Sales and Service depots at*
MANCHESTER
LONDON
EDINBURGH
LEEDS
NEWCASTLE

8.6 LITRE ENGINE: AMPLE POWER AND SPEED WITH ECONOMY. FLUID FLYWHEEL AND PRE-SELECTOR GEARBOX.*

*\* Five-speed gearbox available if required.*

FURTHER PARTICULARS ON REQUEST FROM
TRANSPORT VEHICLES (DAIMLER) LTD., COVENTRY

**Daimler**

*Left* and *Below:* Daimler and Guy were important chassis builders, though they never matched the quantities produced by AEC and Leyland. Daimler had some faithful customers, and in the 1950s it placed fewer adverts than some of its rivals. In this 1950 advert it promotes its single-deck CV series chassis for coaching work. The main picture shows a Duple-bodied CV, the other represents an export coach. Daimler and Guy both tended to be best known for their double-deck models, yet Guy too has chosen to promote its underfloor-engined Arab LUF model, here with an Alexander body for Western SMT.

**PROVED ON THE LONG RUN!**

Over 10,000 miles a month and an average of over 18 miles per gallon are the impressive figures quoted by Western S.M.T. for their "Arab" Lightweights on the Glasgow-London run. These vehicles are part of the large fleet of Guys operated by this company who have recently placed a repeat order for passenger chassis.

**Guy "ARAB" LIGHTWEIGHT**
HEAVYDUTY UNDERFLOOR-ENGINED CHASSIS

**GUY MOTORS LIMITED**
WOLVERHAMPTON & LONDON
Associate Companies: Sunbeam Trolleybus Co. Ltd. & Guy Motors Africa (Pty) Ltd.

CIVIC HALL
LEEDS

LEEDS
HALTON
CROSSGATES **40**

PUA 669

All types of Single
and Double Deck Omnibus
and Coach Bodies

≡ROE≡ *Craftsmen Coachbuilders.*

CHARLES H. ROE LIMITED. CROSSGATES LEEDS
Telephone 45182

*Left:* In 1948/9 AEC had linked up with chassis-builders Crossley and Maudslay and coachbuilders Park Royal and Roe to create the Associated Commercial Vehicles group. Roe was a respected traditional coachbuilder, still building composite (wood and metal) bodies to attractive designs. This 1953 advert shows a Leeds City Transport AEC Regent III; the green second colour offers an approximation of the Leeds livery. It is posed against the Civic Hall in Leeds, underlining a feeling of civic pride.

*Right:* Park Royal had the capacity to accept large orders, including bodies for London Transport, but this 1954 Christmas advert features line illustrations of deliveries for other British customers — an East Kent Guy Arab IV, a Birch Bros AEC Reliance with Royalist coach body and a Northern General AEC/Park Royal Monocoach. Coaches were not a Park Royal speciality, and the Royalist was not a big seller; the Monocoach was an integral bus that was quickly overtaken by AEC's Reliance chassis.

PARK ROYAL VEHICLES LTD
*Extend to all their friends Sincere
Wishes for a Happy Christmas and
a Prosperous New Year*
*1955*

ALL THAT
IS BEST
IN
COACHWORK

PARK ROYAL VEHICLES LTD
PARK ROYAL · LONDON · ENGLAND    PHONE: ELGAR 6522

Left: Metro-Cammell Weymann (MCW) was another major force in the bus-bodybuilding market, a selling organisation representing two established firms, Metro-Cammell and Weymann. Metro-Cammell was a pioneer of metal bodies and in 1952 introduced the ultra-lightweight Orion body. This 1953 advert shows the prototype, on Daimler CLG5 chassis; the body weighed less than two tons, while the whole bus weighed little more than six tons. Red was a popular second colour in 1950s advertising and was not inappropriate for this Potteries bus.

Right: This 1956 advertisement also shows a Potteries bus, but the MCW logo has been applied by the art department. It features the first 30ft-long Orion body, on Leyland Titan PD3 chassis, where the body weight was still low at two-and-a-half tons. The design of the Orion had changed; only the prototype had equal-depth windows on both decks, and the 1956 bus was unusual too in having a six-bay window layout. Production buses had five bay bodies, which gave the bodies less of a multi-windowed appearance.

*1957 Duple-Bedford Super-Vega at Harrow-on-the-Hill*

Above and *Right:* In the days when every coach delivered to a British operator was built in Britain, Duple was the market-leading coachbuilder. Before the war it had developed a relationship with Bedford, and the Bedford/Duple combination became popular with operators of all sizes. The 1956 advertisement features the Duple Super Vega body on Bedford SB chassis, an inexpensive lighter-weight 41-seater. Unusually, it uses a proper colour photo. Although Plaxton would eventually overtake Duple to become market leader, in the 1950s it was still a relatively small firm. The 1953 Plaxton advertisement shows a Venturer body, again on Bedford SB chassis.

34

*Left:* The UK's trolleybus population was beginning to wane in the 1950s, but the trolleybus builders continued to advertise their products from time to time. British United Traction (BUT) had been formed by AEC and Leyland in 1946 to market their existing models, and this 1951 advert uses photos of deliveries to different operators under a slightly dodgy headline. In truth, not all of the models shown are 'real' BUTs; the London bus is an 11-year-old Leyland.

*Right:* This 1955 Sunbeam advert recognises the fact that the 22 F4A models delivered to Walsall Corporation from 1954 were the first 30ft-long two-axle double-deckers for a UK operator; special dispensation was granted at a time when 27ft was the maximum length — although 30ft double-deckers were permitted from 1956. The Walsall buses had Willowbrook bodywork.

# Taking the waters

As its name implies, Llandrindod Wells is a spa town linked with health-giving waters and is a popular destination for tourists visiting the Heart of Wales. **Richard Walters** spent three days there in July 2010.

*All photographs by the author*

*Above:* Sargeants of Kington has bought a number of new Optares in recent years, including this 43-seat Tempo, seen on the service linking Llandrindod Wells with Hereford. The bus was new in 2008 as an Optare demonstrator.

*Left:* New to Sargeants in 2009 was this 33-seat Optare Solo M950. It is seen on the service operating between Llandrindod Wells and Kington via Presteigne, which runs once a day in each direction.

*Above:* Veolia was one of the major operators in the area in 2010. The corporate livery promotes Veolia, but the legal lettering on this 1995 Plaxton-bodied Dennis Javelin identifies the owner as Bebb Travel of Nantgarw.

*Below:* Also owned by Veolia/Bebb is this VDL SB200 with Plaxton Centro body, one of five delivered in 2007. It is seen outside the railway station.

*Left:* An unusual type in the Veolia fleet is this Iveco EuroMidi CC100 with 29-seat Indcar Maxim 2 body — perhaps a Bedford OB for the 21st century.

*Right:* The Traws-Cambria 704 service runs from Newton to Brecon and is operated by Stagecoach. It is a two-hour trip, end to end, Llandrindod Wells being the midway point. This 12.6m Optare Tempo is one of three used on the route by Stagecoach.

*Left:* Local coach operator Weales Wheels runs this rare short-wheelbase Dennis Lancet with UVG bodywork. It was new to the Ministry of Defence.

*Above:* Among coaches visiting the town was this Sunsundegui-bodied Volvo B12B operated by Ambassador Travel of Great Yarmouth on behalf of Grand UK Holidays. It was new in 2008.

*Below:* An impressive Irizar-bodied Scania K340 of Yeomans Travel of Hereford. New in 2009, it is a 49-seater.

# When British buses became less British

*Buses* editor **Alan Millar** explores the growing foreign ownership of Britain's buses.

What you are about to read is a statement of fact and not a party-political declaration, for *Buses Yearbook* caters for readers of all political persuasions and none. Nor is it an expression of Little British nationalism or jingoism.

The bald fact is that by the beginning of 2011 substantial parts of the British bus-operating industry — especially in London — were in German, French, Dutch and Singapore ownership. Not only that, but most of those British operators were once owned by the British state or local authorities, and many of the new owners belong directly or indirectly to foreign governments and taxpayers.

This is not a situation confined to our buses or indeed to our trains, many of which are part of those same foreign-based organisations. Consider, for example, that what used to be the state-owned South Eastern, South Western and London Electricity Boards — and the UK's nuclear power stations — all now belong to EdF Energy, otherwise known as Electricité de France, a business wholly owned by the French state.

For one of the more unexpected — possibly least intended — consequences of the past 30 years of political change either side of the English Channel has been for Britain to privatise many of its publicly owned utilities and monopolies yet ultimately allow state-owned foreign enterprises to acquire several of those privatised organisations. Successive UK governments may believe that these are markets in which this state should have no ownership, but they have shown themselves to be relaxed about other states owning such businesses within our shores.

As I said at the outset, this is what has happened, and *Buses Yearbook* is not the place to debate whether it is right or wrong. It is, however, a place to explain what has happened and how this has changed the structure of our bus industry.

It is worth adding that this is not a new development, nor has the takeover traffic been one-way. The forerunner of what became London Transport's bus operation, the London General Omnibus Company, started life in 1855 as the French-owned Compagnie Générale des Omnibus de Londres. And as I write this in early 2011 the four largest UK-owned bus and rail groups — First, Stagecoach, Go-Ahead and National Express — all have overseas interests, primarily in the United States.

There also have been small-scale examples of privatised British bus operations passing back into different parts of the British public sector. Council-owned Reading Transport bought part of The Bee Line, privatised in the late-1980s National Bus Company sell-off, while council-owned Blackpool Transport bought Fylde Blue Buses soon after the latter was sold by the neighbouring local authority. And perhaps closest to what has happened to some of our businesses — but on a fraction of the scale — council-owned Kingston-upon-Hull City Transport briefly owned Voyages National, a French coach company set up by NBC towards the end of its existence.

## The start of the French connection

So what is the scale of foreign ownership? Of 12 London Buses subsidiaries privatised in 1992 and 1994, seven were foreign-owned by the start of 2011, while two others were in foreign ownership between 2006 and 2010.

By 2011 foreign-owned companies provided around 47% of all tendered London bus services. In another of our major cities — Liverpool — the major bus and rail operators belonged respectively to state-owned German and Dutch transport undertakings.

Outside London, overseas businesses owned the successors to 15 NBC, two Scottish Bus Group, 10 municipal and one PTE undertaking, in addition to other companies either acquired by them or started from scratch. In all, we are talking of approximately 10,000 buses and coaches spread between Kent, South Wales and Scotland, around 4,300 of them in London. French-owned companies have around

1,900 of those buses. Their involvement in the UK goes back farthest — to 1997 — and is easily the most complicated part of this story.

Most local public transport in France — everywhere except Paris and Marseilles — is franchised by competitive tender to commercially structured companies, most of which are French. As European transport markets are gradually opened to international competition, operators can no longer assume that they are immune to attack. And with UK- and Scandinavian-owned groups starting to examine possibilities in other parts of Europe, the French companies began to explore opportunities beyond their boundaries. Given the nature of their home market, it stands to reason that their greatest interest in the UK is where buses or coaches operate in a similar regime with guaranteed regular income — either in the tendered London bus network, providing supported services for local authorities elsewhere in Britain or operating coaches for National Express.

No great surprise, then, that the first French move was to acquire a recently privatised London bus company. London United Busways, serving South West London, was one of 11 (soon reduced to 10) companies created in 1989 when London Buses split its operations into locally managed businesses as a prelude to privatisation and possible deregulation. A former NBC manager, David

Humphrey, had been appointed Managing Director and London United and led a management/employee buyout when these 10 companies were privatised in 1994. Three others went in similar buyouts, and all four sold out within six years.

In September 1995 London United acquired Westlink, a smaller former London Buses subsidiary that had begun life three years before the 1989 break-up as a low-cost subsidiary to compete against outside bidders as routes were offered for tender. It served part of London United's territory and was sold to its management in January 1994 — eight months before any of the big companies were sold. Westlink's independence was short lived, as West Midlands Travel acquired it only 12 weeks later.

London United's independence ended in August 1997 when it accepted a £40 million offer from Transdev, a state-owned company making its first move outside France. At the time, it operated buses in 60 centres as well as the Strasbourg tramway, which had opened in 1994, and it has since expanded into Australia, Spain, Portugal, Italy, the Netherlands and Germany. By 2009 20% of its operations were outside France, and it was the fourth-largest public transport operator in Europe.

Transdev's next step in the UK came early in 2000, when it acquired an 18% shareholding in

*Left:* A London United Wright Crusader-bodied Dennis Dart SLF new in 1996, the year before Transdev acquired the company. It retained this red and grey livery until Transdev applied its corporate fleetnames and Transport for London phased out relief colours in favour of all-over red. These eight buses would be cascaded to Yellow Buses in Bournemouth after Transdev acquired control of that company. ALAN MILLAR

Nottingham City Transport, which remains in local authority control and whose buses — even 18% of them — are excluded from the quoted total of roughly 10,000 buses in foreign ownership. The deal was purely financial. NCT and Transdev were part of the consortium responsible for building and operating Nottingham Express Transit, the tramway opened in the city in 2004, and integrating it with the bus network; NCT needed to raise additional equity without harming its ability to renew its bus fleet, hence the French shareholding.

French expansion in the UK could have happened a lot faster around then, thanks to a hostile takeover bid by Transdev's parent company. In 2000 Caisse des Depots et Consignations (sometimes abbreviated to C3D), an investment company created in 1816 following the fall of Napoleon to safeguard public funds including civil servants' pension funds, bid to buy Go-Ahead Group. The smallest of the UK's City-listed bus and train groups, Go-Ahead was already involved in a joint venture with another French company — railway owned Via-Carianne — in the operation of some British train franchises. C3D failed to win over sufficient Go-Ahead shareholders, and its chances were further undermined by the UK government's securing European Commission approval to refer any such takeover to our competition authorities.

Transdev played a longer game, expanding London United as the London bus network steadily grew bigger in the early years of the new century. Along the way, in 2003, it made a significant acquisition when it bought London Sovereign, serving the capital's north-western and northern suburbs, from Blazefield.

## The birth of Blazefield

Blazefield grew out of the privatisation and subsequent break-up of NBC's West Yorkshire Road Car Co. Alan Stephenson, Managing Director of East Yorkshire Motor Services, had bought West Yorkshire in August 1987 and followed this in March 1988 by acquiring one of NBC's greater basket-cases, London Country North East. He restructured both companies into smaller units, selling some quickly, and in August 1991 sold most of what was left to Blazefield, newly created by co-directors Giles Fearnley and Stuart Wilde.

In Yorkshire Blazefield's main businesses were Harrogate & District, Keighley & District and Yorkshire Coastliner. In the south it inherited Sovereign Bus & Coach, created out of the western part of London Country North East, and Sovereign Buses (Harrow), formed in 1990 to operate 27 midibuses on London Transport tendered services. The Harrow company was maintained as a separate entity in order to ring-fence its profits and prevent Sovereign from using it to cross-subsidise the still fragile main part of the business in Hertfordshire.

In July 1994 Blazefield acquired BTS Coaches, which ran two tendered London routes. BTS stood for Borehamwood Travel Services, and the combined operation subsequently became London Sovereign. Although it thrived by driving up quality in the deregulated bus market, especially in Yorkshire, Blazefield struggled to make London Sovereign work and was as unhappy with the Transport for London contract regime as TfL was unhappy with its performance, hence the sale to Transdev.

Blazefield had long entertained ambitions of expanding across the Pennines into east Lancashire, where it viewed the council-owned Rossendale,

*Left:* **A Scania OmniCity double-decker of Transdev London operating for the London Sovereign part of the business.** **RICHARD GODFREY**

Burnley & Pendle, Hyndburn and Blackburn companies as potential acquisition opportunities. Stagecoach, which acquired Ribble from its ex-NBC managers in 1989, had begun this process by mopping up Burnley & Pendle and the wreckage of Hyndburn (formerly Accrington Corporation) but by 2001 was having a miserable time in east Lancashire. Attempts by Stagecoach to impose its culture, values and pay scales on the former municipal operation at Burnley & Pendle were going badly. Blazefield, however, was prepared to give things a go and took over the depots at Blackburn, Burnley, Bolton and Clitheroe, along with a ragbag of non-standard and in some cases worn-out buses that would soon be replaced by new vehicles. It revived Burnley & Pendle as a separate company and branded the rest with another traditional name, Lancashire United. Such were the sentiments of staff that some symbolically burned their Stagecoach uniforms on the day Blazefield took over. Not that the new owners were frightened to be ruthless. They axed several under-performing routes, focused investment on key corridors and sold the Bolton operation to Blue Bus, which later sold out to Arriva.

Expansion in the North was accompanied by retrenchment in the South, Blazefield eventually offloading all its Hertfordshire and Cambridgeshire businesses in stages to Arriva, National Express, Cavalier Contracts and Centrebus. Although nowhere near conventional retirement age, owners Fearnley and Wilde were keen to ensure management succession for the remainder of the business and to cash in on their investment while they still had time to enjoy it and invest in other activities.

Contact established by the sale of London Sovereign led to Transdev's acquisition in January 2006 of Blazefield's Yorkshire and Lancashire operations, although the former owners were to stay on for a couple of years to help maintain business much as usual. Only three weeks earlier, and after much negotiation and local controversy, Transdev had acquired from Bournemouth Council a 90% shareholding in Yellow Buses. Thus, in the space of a month, it gained valuable expertise in running buses commercially in deregulated British markets some 300 miles apart.

A year after the Blazefield takeover the former owners finally realised another ambition, when Lancashire United acquired Blackburn Transport from Blackburn with Darwen Council. It pleased Giles Fearnley to observe that in 1939 his grandfather, Sheffield Transport General Manager A. R. Fearnley, had produced a report recommending that the Blackburn, Darwen and Accrington undertakings be merged and that they take over Ribble's services in their area. French capital had helped complete this process 68 years later.

Transdev began raising its profile internationally in 2006, adding its name in corporate style to local trading names in the UK, France and everywhere else it had majority shareholdings. In London it dropped the local names altogether, branding its buses simply as Transdev.

In November 2009 it further expanded its London operations by acquiring the tendered operations of NSL Services, formerly part of National Car Parks and one of few smaller operators still providing 'red bus' services. Incorporated into London Sovereign, it took Transdev's British bus fleet to just shy of 1,500 vehicles.

*Right:* **The Blackburn Transport fleet acquired by Transdev Lancashire United included some ECW-bodied long-wheelbase Leyland Olympians new to Lothian. Although painted in the Blazefield companies' yellow school-bus livery, this one was photographed operating an evening peak journey on a public service in 2010, by which time it was 26 years old. GRAHAM ASHWORTH**

## The Transdev/Veolia merger

By now bigger corporate changes were afoot, and in March 2011 Transdev completed a merger with fellow French transport giant Veolia to create Veolia Transdev, a new global force in public transport provision, with 117,000 employees in 28 countries. As part of the process it has also been involved in an amicable divorce, because RATP, the French state-owned operator of buses, trams and Paris Metro trains, held a 25.6% shareholding in Transdev as part of its own global growth ambitions. RATP is remaining apart from the Veolia-controlled Transdev/Veolia merger, and, rather than sell its shareholding in Transdev, agreed to a deal whereby its RATP Dev subsidiary would acquire Transdev assets equal to its value.

Around 3,000 vehicles transferred to RATP Dev, roughly one third of them in the UK, where the deal gave it Yellow Buses, London United and the former NSL Services but not the rest of London Sovereign, which remains with Veolia Transdev, along with the Blazefield businesses in Yorkshire and Lancashire. RATP Dev also acquired businesses in Italy,

Switzerland and parts of France. At the same time as these deals were being completed it purchased, from Ensignbus, the Bath Bus Company's 30-vehicle City Sightseeing business, with operations in Cardiff, Eastbourne and Windsor as well as its home city. RATP Dev already owned L'Open Tour, one of the double-deck sightseeing operators in Paris.

Excluded from the Veolia Transdev merger were Veolia's rapidly reduced bus and coach operations across England and Wales, the senior French partner in the new enterprise having had a chequered, frequently puzzling and less than glorious career in Britain's public transport.

Like C3D, Veolia is a business with 19th-century origins. It commenced trading in 1853 as Compagnie Générale des Eaux (CGE), a water-supply company created by an Imperial decree of Napoleon III. It diversified and expanded in 1980, acquiring Compagnie Générale d'Entreprises Automobiles (CGEA), which took it into transport, waste management and refuse collection. Three years later CGE began moving into the film and television business, and in 1998 it renamed itself Vivendi. In 2000 it split in two, the CGEA part becoming Veolia.

CGEA had adopted two trading names — Onyx for waste management and refuse collection, Connex for public transport — and it was as Connex that it first sprang to British attention, in October 1996, winning the franchises awarded for the South Central and South Eastern rail networks radiating from London. These were 10- and 15-

*Right:* Transdev has added several batches of Optare single-deckers to the Yellow Buses fleet in Bournemouth, among them this Versa. **STEPHEN WHITELEY**

year franchises, and presumably everyone involved was confident that this would be the start of something big and good.

But it all went badly wrong. Both franchises were withdrawn early, Connex losing the re-tendered South Central routes to GoVia — the Go-Ahead/Via Carianne joint venture — in 2001, while South Eastern reverted to state ownership from November 2003, when a Strategic Rail Authority company took over temporary operation, before GoVia eventually won a long-term contract. The SRA questioned Connex's financial management and wider ability to run the business, showing itself clearly in no hurry to let Connex near any more of the nation's trains. This was unprecedented action, and nothing like it has happened since to any train operator.

By this time Connex had also established itself as a British bus operator, winning its first two London bus contracts, which it started operating during 2000 from a new depot in Croydon. It also bought second-hand buses for a rail-replacement fleet and used the railway station yard at Lewes for a feeder bus service from Uckfield that became the nucleus for a group of tendered rural services in Sussex. After losing the South Central franchise it closed the Lewes base early in 2001, transferring the staff and contracts to local independent operator RDH Services.

The London operation continued to grow, partly by winning tenders and also by taking over seven routes, 84 buses and the Battersea depot of Limebourne, another TfL contractor, in July 2001. Limebourne had been part of Q Drive, which collapsed in 1998, and had been rescued by its management, which in August 2000 acquired one of National Express Group's short-lived ventures into London bus operation. Like a later venture we shall meet in this story, this was called Travel London,

and operated two routes using Optare single-deckers.

By the time Connex was called in, TfL was desperate. Limebourne had a poor reputation for quality, in terms of service reliability and its relatively poorly paid staff. Had the French not been prepared to take it on, the expectation had been that TfL would set up its own direct operation in the mould of its East Thames subsidiary. Perhaps TfL and the SRA viewed things differently, or perhaps Connex's bus and rail businesses were very different, but it seems ironic that one public body should have trusted the company to take on a problem operator whilst the other felt the need to assume direct operation of its services.

Connex Bus was no picnic. It bid low to win TfL contracts and failed to secure sufficient volume of work to be profitable. And its combination of new-start contracts at the Croydon base and the toxic mixture of the troubled Limebourne and Travel London operations at Battersea did nothing to promote a forward-looking cohesive culture. Having been sent packing tout de suite by the SRA, Connex had little stomach for continued operation of London buses, and it came as little surprise when, in February 2004, the loss-making venture was handed to National Express for what at the time was described as a 'nominal consideration'. Its 12 routes, 200 buses, 700 staff and two depots transferred to the second incarnation of Travel London, of which more later.

There was one other Connex operation left in the British Isles, a 10-year franchise taken up in 2002 to run the public bus service in Jersey. It was managed from France — which, after all, is geographically closer than England is to Jersey. That operation has continued to trade as Connex, even though Veolia Transport has since been adopted as the name

*Right:* An Optare Solo for Connex's London fleet, photographed in Leeds before delivery.
OPTARE

across just about every other part of the global public transport business except Lebanon, where there are Connex school buses.

### Veolia's British comeback

It was as Veolia that the company tried to rehabilitate itself in the UK transport market. As early as 2003 it recruited as its UK Managing Director John O'Brien, formerly Franchise Director at the Office of Rail Franchising, and hit upon a strategy of building up a quality bus and coach business it intended would be so good that Veolia would once again be considered worthy of running trains.

Between October 2005 and November 2007 it made eight such acquisitions in England and Wales, starting with Bebb Travel of Llantwit Fardre, which ran contracted local buses and National Express coaches. The other South Wales purchases were of Pullman, Long's and Hawkes in the Swansea area and Clayton Jones' Shamrock Travel group serving Pontypridd, Cardiff, Barry and Newport. Its biggest English purchase, in March 2006, was of Dunn-Line, the Nottingham-based group listed on the Alternative Investment Market and which had expanded north and south, as well as making its first overseas acquisition of a bus company in Poland. Veolia subsequently acquired Paul James Coaches in Leicestershire and Astons of Kempsey in Worcestershire.

The Dunn-Line and Shamrock purchases alone cost Veolia nearly £20 million, and the industry was rife with reports of family-owned businesses being offered mouth-watering sums that translated into temptingly generous retirement pension funds. I have it on impeccable authority that First's purchase of Truronian in 2008 was at least partly a strategic move to prevent Veolia from establishing itself in Cornwall.

Besides these acquisitions Veolia won contracts and established a base in York in February 2007

and two months later secured National Express contracts for coach services from Birmingham, taking over a directly operated NatEx fleet and some contracts held by the Birmingham Coach Company, then owned by Go-Ahead. The Welsh business bid robustly for tendered services, winning substantial Mid Wales contracts from Powys Council, and the Dunn-Line operation expanded similarly in Nottinghamshire and South Yorkshire.

Then the tide turned as rapidly as Veolia had built up its patchwork of businesses. The York operation was sold to Transdev in August 2008, and the following March Dunn-Line's Hull business went to East Yorkshire. During its build-up phase Veolia had made a tentative takeover approach to East Yorkshire, which politely declined but expressed interest in buying the Hull operation, should the French ever wish to sell.

Other bits of Dunn-Line have also gone — Lincoln depot in 2008, Tuxford (Nottinghamshire) in 2010 and Nottingham early in 2011. Some of the Nottingham and Tuxford work — including National Express coach contracts — was taken on by Your Bus, a new Dunn-family business set up in June 2009. And poor performance in Wales led the traffic commissioner to cut the Veolia Transport Cymru operator-licence authorisation by 119, to 277, in December 2010.

Not that the rather sorry story of Veolia's UK bus and coach operations should mislead you into thinking this is a bit player elsewhere. Far from it. Besides France, where it has bus, tram, train and ferry interests, and Lebanon, already mentioned, Veolia operates buses in Belgium, Germany, the Netherlands, Norway, Sweden, Finland, Spain, the Czech Republic, Slovakia, Poland, Serbia, Slovenia, the USA (including Alexander Dennis Enviro500 double-deckers in Las Vegas), Canada, Australia, Chile, Colombia and Israel. In several of these countries it acquired newly privatised operators — an opportunity denied it in the UK, where most fleets, owned hitherto by the state or local authorities, were already in private ownership.

In 2009 Veolia had more than 37,000 vehicles and 77,500 employees in 28 countries. Of these, nearly 15,000 vehicles and 31,700 employees were in France.

### The Kéolis connection

One other significant French player, Kéolis, has dabbled in the British bus market. The largest public transport provider in France, with interests in Sweden, Denmark, the Netherlands, Belgium, Germany, Canada and the United States, this operator of 15,800 buses and coaches was known previously as Via-Carianne — the 'Via' in the GoVia joint rail venture that runs the Southern, Southeastern and London Midland train franchises in England and which is majority-owned by the French state railway, SNCF. It also is a joint-venture partner with FirstGroup in the Transpennine Express rail franchise.

Early in 2010 Kéolis and Arriva discussed a possible merger, joint venture or French takeover; this came to nothing but could have transformed the French presence in the UK public transport business. The earlier Kéolis involvement lasted from 2001 to 2008, during which time it had a 20% shareholding in Eastbourne Buses, which 50-vehicle operation was the smallest arm's-length municipal bus company in England. In a move its partners hoped would lead to bigger things in Eastbourne and beyond, the borough council kept control of its flagging bus company with the aid of outside capital.

Had Eastbourne Buses met a complex set of targets, Kéolis would have increased its shareholding to a maximum of 49% by 2006 at the earliest. And had this proved a resounding success, Kéolis hoped to sell similar partnerships to other surviving municipal bus companies. None of that happened, partly because of the arrival of Cavendish Motor Services, a new direct competitor set up by Renown Coaches and a former Eastbourne managing director. With Eastbourne Buses in financial trouble, the council offered it for sale, buying back the 20% shareholding from Kéolis just before concluding a deal to sell 100% of the business to Stagecoach, which also bought Cavendish.

Just like Veolia in the UK, Kéolis is bigger and better beyond Eastbourne than this unfortunate episode turned out. It just did not back a winner.

### Travel London goes Dutch

Which brings us back to somewhere this story has taken us twice already — Travel London. By 2009, having made expensive acquisitions in Spain that transformed the Spanish Cosmen family into its largest single shareholder, National Express was running into financial problems and needed to sell assets to survive. It would eventually receive unwelcome takeover approaches from First and Stagecoach, which it warded off by the skin of a few teeth and, in the latter case, despite the Cosmens' support for such a deal.

The biggest asset sold was Travel London, which by now had grown to a profitable 470-vehicle fleet thanks to the purchase of the London and Surrey tendered bus operations of Tellings Golden Miller, and for which additional contract wins would soon take it to 500. The buyer, in May 2009, was NedRailways, a trading division of Nederlandse Spoorwegen (NS), the Dutch state railway, which paid £32 million to NatEx in much-needed cash. NedRailways, like Connex before it, was already established on the British railway network, having

*Right:* Veolia was particularly interested in higher-quality contracts, such as this park-and-ride service in Swansea, operated by new Optare Tempos in a dedicated livery. ALAN MILLAR

*Left:* This Alexander-bodied Volvo Olympian has seen service with two of the overseas groups now operating in the UK. It was new to Singapore Bus Services and was a solitary example imported by Metroline after the ComfortDelGro takeover. It was sold subsequently to Veolia, which in 2009 was operating it on a students' service in Cardiff. BARRIE GILBERT

*Right:* A debris trail of past owners of companies in the Veolia family, seen on the side of a Veolia Cymru bus in Pontypridd in 2010. It was still in Dunn-Line lilac. DAVID JENKINS

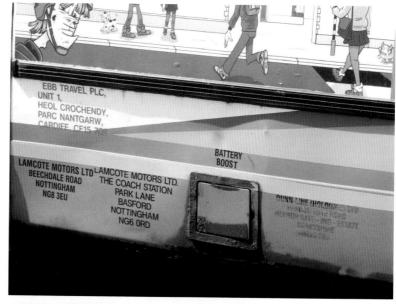

*Left:* A clear British connection on a Veolia bus in the south of France. This is one of four East Lancs Nordic-bodied Volvo B7Ls of its Bus Azur fleet providing an open-top service in Cannes. ALAN MILLAR

*Left:* **An MCV Evolution-bodied MAN of Eastbourne Buses in the final version of the operator's blue livery. MARK LYONS**

run Merseyrail since 2003 and Northern Rail since 2004, both in a joint venture with British facilities-management company Serco.

NedRailways has since renamed itself Abellio — one of those non-specific multi-lingual names (like Arriva or Veolia) that somehow stick in the mind yet say nothing about what the company actually does. Abellio was a 600-vehicle German bus operator bought by NedRailways in 2008 — around the same time as it entered the Czech bus market.

Ironically, this expansion has taken place against a curious turn of events in the Netherlands, where most state- and many local-authority-owned buses have been franchised to Arriva, Veolia and the formerly state-owned Connexxion undertaking, now majority-owned by Transdev. NS, meanwhile, has taken a 49% stake in Qbuzz, a newer Dutch bus company challenging its foreign competitors.

Abellio has ambitions for further growth in the UK but at the time of writing has yet to realise them, perhaps because of the paucity of opportunities to buy businesses on the scale of Travel London, which now trades as Abellio London and Abellio Surrey.

## Arriva bought by Deutsche Bahn

By far the most significant of all the European acquisitions of UK bus companies came in August 2010, when Deutsche Bahn (DB), the German state railway, bought Arriva for £1.58 billion. For the time being, at least, Arriva remains a clearly identifiable British-based and British-managed business that happens to be owned by an arm of the German state rather than shareholders trading on the London Stock Exchange.

For those who cared to consider it, there was a certain inevitability that a German public transport giant should emerge onto a European if not global stage. Germany is Europe's largest economy, and a similar sort of undertaking, Deutsche Post (the privatised German post office), has long since expanded globally through the acquisition of brands like DHL. DB, indeed, describes itself as the world's second-largest transport company — after Deutsche Post.

It was surely inconceivable, once its rail and bus networks were opened up to competitive tendering and potential privatisation, that Germany would leave the pickings entirely to large French and British groups starting to stalk the globe in pursuit of growth opportunities. If any German business

*Right:* **Kéolis livery and logo on a Setra low-floor bus in Lille, northern France. ALAN MILLAR**

*Left:* The Surrey version of Abellio livery on an East Lancs Myllennium-bodied Alexander Dennis Dart owned by Surrey County Council and reallocated from First following the withdrawal of a high-profile school-bus service. The Dutch company's London buses are all-over red. MARK LYONS

was a ready-made public transport giant, it was DB. Besides dominating the country's rail services, various DB subsidiaries operate around 12,500 buses and coaches in Germany, including railway and post-bus operations formed into regional companies in the late 1970s.

No date has yet been set, but the German government intends that DB should ultimately be privatised. Parts of the rail network have already been franchised to other operators, and DB began realising its dreams of bus expansion overseas in 2007 with the acquisition of Danish operator Pan Bus. Attempts to compete for local-transport franchises in France have yet to bear fruit.

DB has been active on Britain's railways since February 2007, when it acquired principal freight operator EWS. Its acquisition of Laing Rail in April 2008 brought with it operation of the Chiltern Railways franchise, along with shareholdings in London Overground and open-access operator Wrexham & Shropshire Railway, which competed in part with Arriva Trains Wales, and since April 2010 it has operated the Tyne & Wear Metro.

Just as DB is the obvious vehicle for German expansion, so Arriva was an ideal candidate for purchase. Alone among the UK public transport groups it established itself across Europe by acquiring bus operators and winning rail franchises. By early 2010 its buses (some operated in joint ventures, as a way of entering markets) could be found in the Netherlands, Denmark, Sweden, Italy, Spain, Portugal, the Czech Republic, Poland, Hungary and Slovakia, and in 2011 it commenced a 10-year franchise to operate buses in Malta. Arriva also built up a 900-bus fleet and a passenger- and freight-train business in Germany, which the European Commission ordered be sold as a condition of the DB takeover; a deal towards the end of 2010 saw this go — for more

than £250 million — to Trenitalia, the Italian state railway, the latter making its first move outside its home country.

### Arriva in the UK

In the UK Arriva has grown to operate 6,300 buses (1,700 in London, where it runs 20% of tendered services), and it is by far the most geographically spread of the foreign-owned UK operators. It also is unique in the accidental manner of its entry into the bus and coach business.

Until 1997 Arriva was known as T. Cowie plc, which commenced trading in 1931 as a family-owned motor-cycle dealer in Sunderland (where Arriva remains based today). It grew to become one of the country's largest car and commercial-vehicle dealers, and in pursuit of further growth of that business in 1980 the by then City-listed group acquired the London-based George Ewer Group, which owned well-known coach operator Grey-Green. Many other groups making similar purchases would have offloaded such a non-core activity at an early opportunity, but Cowie gave it a go, starting a process that would eventually see Arriva quit car retailing.

With the traditional coach market — especially the excursions business, on which Grey-Green had depended for much of its income — in decline, Cowie developed new opportunities and transformed itself increasingly into a bus operator as London routes were offered for competitive tender. It also bought the Hughes DAF coach dealership and rental business and acquired two of the big red London bus companies — Leaside and South London — when London Buses was privatised in 1994.

In 1996 Cowie bought British Bus, which had begun life in the NBC privatisation of 1987/8 as Drawlane Transport before going on to build up regional groupings of ex-NBC, municipal and independent operators in North and Mid Wales and North West, North East and South East England and the Midlands, as well as a much smaller operation in West Scotland that betrayed a failed attempt to create something bigger north of the border.

In 2011 Arriva's British bus operations outside London take in part or all of former NBC subsidiaries Northumbria, United, West Riding/ Yorkshire Woollen, North Western, Crosville, Crosville Wales, Midland Red North, Midland Fox, Luton & District, Maidstone & District and the four companies created by the break-up of London Country. It also owns a remnant of Clydeside Scottish, the former municipal operations in Darlington, Derby, Burton-upon-Trent (latterly East Staffordshire), Colchester, Southend and Maidstone, as well as most of what was once Merseyside PTE.

Besides the above Arriva has Tellings Golden Miller, a business unlike any within the other big British groups. Hitherto a family-owned coach and local-bus operator, it was taken onto the Alternative Investment Market and acquired by Arriva in January 2008. It retains its own identity and includes the former municipal company in Colchester, inherited by Arriva with British Bus and sold to then-independent TGM as a bit of a bad job, only to come back into the fold. In 2010 TGM also assumed control of the one-time London Country operations in Harlow.

Beyond buses, Arriva holds two rail franchises. Arriva Trains Wales covers most routes in and to and from the principality, while CrossCountry is responsible for those stretching across Scotland and England from Aberdeen to Penzance.

DB's stated intention is that Arriva should carry on much as before, as an entrepreneurial business developing its operations in the UK and expanding where opportunities present themselves in Europe. Not having much presence of its own outside Germany, DB can ill-afford to do otherwise, but the real test of how well this strategy works will come after Arriva Chief Executive David Martin — once a finance director within NBC — and other architects of the group's expansion hand over the reins to younger generations.

**From Far East and Down Under**
The other foreign owner of British bus operations is the Singapore-based ComfortDelGro Corporation, formed in 2002 by the merger of DelGro, which already owned 75% of SBS Transit (the Singapore bus and Metro operator), and taxi and private-bus operator Comfort. DelGro sprang to attention in the UK in February 2000, when it announced a £73.8 million takeover of City-listed London bus company Metroline.

One of the four main red bus companies subject to management/employee buyouts in 1994, Harrow-based Metroline was floated on the stock market in July 1997. The following year it made two significant acquisitions, the first seeing it nearly double in size when it bought the neighbouring London Northern company (also a privatised London Buses subsidiary) from MTL, the arm's length bus-operating successor to Merseyside PTE. Today it provides around 13% of London's tendered services and runs around 1,200 buses.

The second deal of 1998 saw Metroline move way out of territory with the acquisition of Scottish Citylink Coaches, the former Scottish Bus Group express-coach operation that National Express had been obliged to sell after winning the ScotRail

*Left:* An Alexander Dennis Enviro300 of Arriva the Shires in Hatfield, on a route taken over with part of Blazefield's Sovereign Bus & Coach business. **ALAN MILLAR**

train-operating franchise. Like National Express, Citylink relied on contractors to provide its services.

Today ComfortDelGro operates around 41,000 buses, coaches and taxis, including black-cab fleets in London and other British cities. It already earns about half of its revenue outside Singapore, the group being involved in wholly owned or joint ventures in Australia, Ireland, China, Vietnam and Malaysia.

The Australian businesses include Westbus, acquired from National Express Group in 2005 and which has a small coach subsidiary in London. The Irish operation is Citylink, an offshoot of the Scottish company set up to compete with Bus Éireann on inter-city routes. There also was a short-lived venture, Aerdart, which Metroline hoped would benefit from liberalisation of the bus network in Dublin; this has yet to happen, however, and Aerdart soon closed.

Among the joint ventures is one in Scotland, where in September 2005 Stagecoach and Scottish Citylink ended several months of hard-fought competition for coach passengers by combining their interests on trunk routes into a company owned 65% by ComfortDelGro and 35% by Stagecoach, which Stagecoach manages on a day-to-day basis.

Stagecoach also figures in the story of London bus companies in foreign ownership. These were East London and Selkent, bought by Stagecoach in the 1994 privatisation for around £140 million. Their sale in 2006 to the Australian-owned Macquarie Bank, for £264 million, allowed Stagecoach to pay off some debts, top up its employees' pension fund and fund

acquisitions of bus companies in the deregulated market outside London. This came about because Macquarie, keen to buy businesses delivering guaranteed and predictable cash earnings, expressed interest in Stagecoach's bus and ferry business in New Zealand. Stagecoach already had a willing New Zealand buyer lined up in the form of Infratil, which had earlier taken its solitary airport — Prestwick, in Scotland — off its hands. But when it dangled the London-bus possibility before their eyes the Australian bankers made an offer the shrewd Scots dared not refuse, and as far as the world was concerned that was the end of Stagecoach operation of regulated buses in London.

Except that Macquarie's stewardship of what became known as the East London Bus Group was less than blissful. Earnings plummeted, and in tougher economic conditions the bus business went up for sale. There was authoritative talk, in the business pages of at least one quality daily, of this being the next British purchase by RATP, but the actual purchaser, in October 2010, turned out to be none other than Stagecoach. It bought ELBG back for a mere £52.8 million — a reflection of the operation's market value and the work needed to restore it to something approaching its former state.

The East London experience probably says nothing for or against foreign ownership of bus companies, but figures like £140 million, £264 million and £52.8 million will likely reinforce a good few prejudices about banks' role — or otherwise — in the global financial downturn of the early 21st century.

*Right:* An Alexander Dennis Enviro400 of Metroline, with the blue skirt introduced when the company was privatised (and subsequently dropped, in the move to all-red buses), at Euston station. PHIL HALEWOOD

## Whatever next?

So where next for the UK bus industry? It would be unwise to predict anything other than that the structure of ownership at home and abroad is unlikely to remain as it is now. The four big groups still City-listed in early 2011 are all still relatively young businesses, none much more than 30 years old and all possibly open to radical change over the next 10 years. For some, that might mean foreign ownership or merger with an overseas player. Much depends too on whether the railways of mainland Europe remain state-owned and whether the French groups continue to dominate their home market.

Crucial to the future is how foreign owners choose to run their British assets. Experience in many businesses — and this applies equally to British companies expanding abroad — reveals that success visits those that employ local managers immersed in the culture and working methods of their country far more often than it does those who parachute in their own people on a world tour.

The story since August 1997 suggests that foreign ownership of part of our industry — especially in London and any other regulated markets — is here to stay, but that some ventures may last longer than others. And if the fashion for names like Abellio, Arriva and Veolia holds up, be ready to familiarise yourself with many more bus companies whose names owe nothing obvious to either the language or geography of their country of origin.

*Left:* East London Bus Group's period of Australian ownership included 2008, at which time Routemaster RM1933 wore this special maroon and platinum livery to mark the centenary of Bow garage. ALAN MILLAR

# Clydebank connection

Clydebank was famous for ships and sewing machines  both industries long since vanished. **Billy Nicol** looks at buses in this modest town northwest of Glasgow.

*Right:* Coach hirer John Morrow began running services in Clydebank in 1988 using route numbers similar to those of former Central SMT services in the town. A Leyland National which had been new to Crosville is seen in 1992. Morrow's local services were sold to Kelvin Central later that year.

*Left:* In 1988 Allander of Milngavie acquired the services of Barrie of Balloch which traded as Loch Lomond Coaches and expanded into Clydebank. The services were sold to Kelvin Central in 1996. This Volvo B10M with Duple Dominant bus body had started life with Hutchison of Overtown.

*Right:* Avondale, one of the many post-deregulation Greenock operators, expanded on the north bank of the River Clyde and then moved its base to Clydebank. Among many Mercedes minibuses operated was this example with Euro Coach Builders bodywork, acquired from Dublin Bus.

*Left:* The lucrative Dumbarton Road corridor, linking Clydebank with Glasgow, has seen much competition. New to London Buses but by now working for PD Travel, this 1990 Dennis Dart with Carlyle body is seen heading for Partick in 2003. PD Travel would cease trading in 2008.

*Right:* John Morrow later returned to local-bus operation and in 2003 was running a fleet consisting mainly of minibuses, including this Mercedes Vario with Plaxton Beaver 2 body. Later purchases would include Optare Solos and short Dennis Darts.

*Above:* McColl's Coaches has operated a variety of services around Clydebank using a mixed fleet including former Travel West Midlands Mercedes minibuses. New in 1997 this 811D with 27-seat Marshall body was photographed in 2004.

*Below:* Although based in Wishaw, to the south-east of Glasgow, McKindless operated services in Clydebank. Acquired from Arriva London, this Plaxton-bodied Dart was photographed in 2005 operating in competition with First Glasgow on a service to Glasgow city centre. This service ceased in February 2010, when the McKindless business closed without warning.

*Right:* Also operating along Dumbarton Road to Partick was DB Travel, which in 2007 was running this Volvo B6, with Alexander Dash body. Most Alexander-bodied B6s were new to Stagecoach, but this vehicle had started life in 1994 with Nottingham City Transport.

*Left:* Glasgow Citybus began operations in 1999 and was soon recognised as a high-quality operator, a position maintained in the ownership of West Coast Motors, which acquired the business in 2006. This is a 2003 DAF SB120 with Wright Cadet body. The company also runs Plaxton-bodied SB120s.

*Right:* Among the more unusual buses to have served in Clydebank is this Volvo B10L with Belfast-built Alexander Ultra body, seen in 2010 running for McColl's. It was one of four acquired from Dublin Bus and was new in 1997. Very few B10Ls have operated in Scotland.

# Classic coaching 60 years ago

**John Hillmer** illustrates a selection of the coaches to be seen on Britain's roads in 1952.

*All photographs from the author's collection*

*Left:* Waiting at the Palace Pier, Brighton, in June 1952 before operating an evening mystery drive to 'Somewhere off the Beaten Track' (according to the advertising board leaning against it) is this delightful Southdown Harrington-bodied Leyland Cub KPZ4, new in 1938. It lasted in service until January 1956. The fare was 3s (15p).

*Below:* In 1949 Hants & Dorset placed in service three Bristol L6Bs with Beadle coach bodywork, the first of which is seen on a day tour to London at Regent's Park. Rebuilt by Hants & Dorset with full-width fronts in the late 1950s, all three would be withdrawn in the early 1960s.

*Left:* A United Welsh Duple-bodied Albion Valkyrie CX13, new in 1948, seen in Exeter alongside a Duple-bodied Bedford WTB of J. Parsons & Sons of Holsworthy, Devon. The WTB was the precursor of the OB; this one had been new to the Royal Air Force in the 1940s and would operate until 1958. The Albion would remain service until early 1960.

*Right:* The Torquay-based coach firm, Grey Cars, was acquired by Devon General in 1932 and was wound up two years later. However, after World War 2 the Grey Cars name was revived and appeared on Devon General coaches. Typifying these is a 1950 Duple-bodied AEC Regal III, one of 12, photographed outside the operator's booking office in Vaughan Parade, Torquay. The slender AEC radiator gave a far more pleasing overall appearance to the vehicle than the rather stubby radiator of the United Welsh Albion in the previous photograph, which carries the same body style.

*Left:* In 1950 a length of 30ft, instead of the previous 27ft 6in, became permissible for two-axle single-deckers. Taking advantage of this is a Royal Blue Duple-bodied Bristol LL6B new the following year and seen in London's Victoria Coach Station in August 1952 on the Southampton service. Alongside is a Thames Valley Bristol KSW6B with lowbridge Eastern Coach Works bodywork, operating the express service to Reading.

*Left:* During the 1950s the ubiquitous Bedford OB was to be found in the Crosville fleet, in bus and coach form. Parked outside Betws-y-Coed railway station in August 1952 is one of 23 OB coaches delivered in 1950, fitted with the customary Duple Vista 29-seat bodywork although with the less common quarter-lights in the roof. Withdrawal came just one year after this photograph was taken, in 1953, when the OB was sold to sister British Transport Commission company Tillings Transport. Most of Crosville's 1950 OBs remained in service until 1958.

*Right:* In 1951 Thames Valley took delivery of a batch of six Bristol LWL6Bs with 30ft-long full-front forward-entrance 37-seat coach bodies by Eastern Coach Works. In 1959 nine similar vehicles, also new in 1951, were acquired from United Counties. This coach would be withdrawn by Thames Valley in 1964.

*Below:* The introduction of the Bedford SB and Commer Avenger forward-control chassis saw full-front bodywork become commonplace on lightweight coaches. The chassis builders would supply the front scuttle assembly, as used on their goods models, which was incorporated into the body design. Norwich bodybuilder Churchill was recommended by Commer and, by use of an aluminium strip, neatly blended the Commer grille into the front mudguards, producing a very attractive design. Demonstrating this is a 1950 Avenger 34-seater operated by Barton Transport, photographed on tour in Chester. The letter P above the fleet number reminded the refueller that the vehicle was petrol-engined.

*Right:* The SB, Bedford's first forward-control design, was launched at the 1950 Commercial Motor Show as the replacement for the OB and, as a 33-seater, was the company's largest design to date. Early examples had the bulbous front cowl of the contemporary Bedford lorry incorporated into the bodybuilder's own design, as seen on this 1952 coach operated by Bullock of Cheadle; it had a Duple Vega body and was photographed in Chester just a few weeks after entering service. The SB in all its variations was to become the longest-running Bedford PSV chassis, surviving until the end of Bedford production in 1987.

*Left:* Unlike Bullock's Bedford SB this coach in the fleet of Smiths of Wigan gives no clue to the chassis make. New in February 1950, it is a Leyland Tiger PS1 with a 31-seat body by Bellhouse Hartwell of Westhoughton, near Bolton. It is seen passing Chester Cathedral in July 1952.

*Below:* Robertson, of Longham, Dorset, who traded as Rambler, operated this Dennis Lancet J3 with 35-seat Whitson bodywork. It was new in October 1947. James Whitson & Co, based in West Drayton, Middlesex, had a patented flush-fitting sliding passenger door which, when closed, gave an attractive smooth-flowing line to the bodywork which is seen to good advantage in this view at Victoria Coach Station. The coach would later pass to Bere Regis & District Motor Services, which took over the Rambler business in 1952.

*Above:* This Austin CXB of Rhyl United Coachways had 29-seat bodywork by Rochdale coachbuilder Trans-United. New in January 1950, it is seen in the coach park in Caernarvon, with the castle walls dominating the background. Introduced in 1947, the CXB was Austin's answer to the Bedford OB and was sometimes called the 'Birmingham Bedford', as it was built at Austin's Longbridge factory in the city.

*Below:* Also an Austin, but a forward-control model, is this odd-looking coach of Pye's Motor Tours, Llandudno, photographed in Betws-y-Coed. New in July 1949, it had 31-seat bodywork by Mann Egerton, a company involved primarily in the car trade, with a major Austin agency for the Norwich area. At the end of the war it had taken on body reconditioning for London Transport, which led to orders for some 130 single-deck 31-seat bus bodies, but more in keeping with the company's principal business was the building of bodies on Austin chassis. The body design shown here utilised the style of grille from Austin's 30cwt Three-Way van. Note the semaphore indicator operating as the vehicle pulls into its parking space.

*Above:* Midland Red had always been at the cutting edge of bus and coach technology and demonstrated this again when, in 1948/9, it placed in service a batch of 45 underfloor-engined coaches which were based on its S6-class single-deck service bus. They were designated C1 and had 30-seat bodywork by Duple to Midland Red design, incorporating a central sliding entrance door and, unusually for a coach, a recessed driver's windscreen. Most C1s remained in service until 1965, and a few gained an extended lease of life as training buses, surviving thus into the 1970s.

*Below:* Among the most successful of the early underfloor-engined chassis was the Leyland Royal Tiger, for which Ribble was the largest customer, taking both bus and coach versions. This is one of 120 Leyland-bodied PSU1/15 centre-entrance coaches, all new in 1951, outside the operator's depot in Foundry Hill, Blackburn, during an Omnibus Society visit.

# Not so misguided

**David Cole** considers Birmingham's guided busway — the first in the world to be operated by double-deckers.

The year 2012 marks a quarter of a century since service ceased on Britain's first modern guided busway, which was also the first in the world to feature double-deck operation. Looking back, there can be little doubt that the short installation deep in Birmingham's northern suburbs was anything but a demonstration project; it was a pilot, the start of the future — but this was a future soon to change radically with deregulation. Once the Birmingham guided busway disappeared it seemed to be formally 'forgotten' and was probably not given the appropriate credit when the technology was applied to later projects.

### The case for guided busways

Reversing the decline in public transport use has been the challenge for transport professionals for nearly half a century. The growth in car ownership and changing lifestyles have continued to reduce patronage in many areas, but there have been notable successes. In recent years enlightened cities such as Brighton and Cambridge have shown what the bus can do, but back in the 1970s and '80s it was rail-based schemes that appeared to make the running.

Established in the late 1960s, most Passenger Transport Authorities were looking to their Executives to deliver modern fast transport networks which would be unaffected by growing traffic congestion. The metro concept, featuring underground stations in city centres, was popular, although only the Tyne & Wear PTE network was realised, other PTE areas eventually changing their focus to deliver surface-running modern tramways nearly 20 years later. 'Heavy' rail was also a key focus, Merseyside and West Midlands being amongst the PTEs to deliver significant improvements to services. The Cross-City line in Birmingham, opened in 1978, demonstrated that fixed-infrastructure services were capable of attracting significant growth in public transport usage, even if the initial rolling stock was close to life-expired.

So what is it about fixed infrastructure that generates custom? It probably includes prominence of the infrastructure, which provides a continuous reminder of the public transport opportunity and a perception of permanence from the investment, as well as the faster journey times expected. Together with appropriate fare schemes these attributes give public transport a chance to break ingrained travel patterns. But fixed-infrastructure schemes are extremely expensive. Combining the flexibility of the bus with a fixed infrastructure appeared to offer the best of both worlds, and by the early 1980s the technology was sufficiently advanced for this to be put into practice.

### Developing technology

As early as the late 1920s the LMS railway recognised the benefits of a vehicle that could run on roads and fixed track. The Karrier 'ro-railer' bus was tested around Stratford-upon-Avon, the flexibility of use being achieved by retractable rail wheels in a manner similar to that employed on support vehicles used by railways and tramways today. The operation faded away, but around a quarter of a century later a similar concept was trialled in Germany, this time using a separate bogie for the main rail wheels, reducing the on-road weight. Again, the operation faded out, although a vehicle survives in preservation.

Meanwhile, in France, development of pneumatic-tyred trains was advancing. Line 11 of the Paris Metro was reopened in 1956 with pneumatic tyres both on the driven/carrying wheels and on the horizontal guidance wheels, although normal steel wheels and rails were retained for switching purposes. Fixed-infrastructure systems no longer meant only steel wheels on steel rails, and the Germans were to lead the way in applying external mechanical guidance systems to otherwise standard buses. In 1980 Mercedes-Benz launched its O-Bahn concept with a trial installation sharing a metre-gauge tramway reservation in Essen.

Essen's initial vehicles were standard Mercedes-Benz O.305 single-deckers equipped with guide wheels, and the short length of guided busway

enabled them to avoid local congestion as well as prove the technology. Attracting interest from around the world, the trial was obviously successful, Essen deciding on significant expansion. This included not only the conversion of a reserved-track median-strip tramway that was in need of refurbishment but also the equipping of the city-centre tramway subways for joint operation by trams and guided 'duo-buses'. These latter were less successful than expected, and the guided buses reverted to surface operation in diesel mode.

A significant opportunity to demonstrate the flexibility of the O-Bahn concept was presented by the selection of this system to upgrade an important public transport corridor in Adelaide, South Australia. Routes operated in conventional mode in the city and outer suburbs were bundled onto a guided busway along a dried-up riverbed, providing a faster service through the core of the corridor where extension to the city's tramway network would not have been viable.

**The West Midlands demonstration scheme**
Amongst the international visitors to the Essen system were representatives from the West Midlands PTA and PTE, who viewed the adaptation of abandoned tram reservations for guided buses as a means of addressing growing traffic congestion in Birmingham. Ideally the long stretches of reservation along the busy Bristol Road would have been chosen, but to derive significant benefit major works would have been required

to reduce the pinch-points through suburban shopping centres, where trams had shared the roadway with other vehicles.

Following the consideration of a number of alternatives the choice fell on the short section of reservation in Streetly Road between Stockland Green and Short Heath, in Birmingham's northern suburbs. The tramway system had reached Stockland Green in 1912, was extended over this 600yd extension as service 78 in 1926 and survived until the final closure of Birmingham trams in July 1953. The replacement buses on route 65 used the relatively quiet carriageways either side of the reservation, which was grassed over. Key benefits of choosing Streetly Road included the fact that it was served by a single route, minimising vehicle requirements, and its relative obscurity; unlike most of Birmingham's tramway reservations this was not on a main arterial road.

The choice was not so popular with some members of the local community, who campaigned against the loss of around 50 mature trees which once screened the tramway. They were answered by a PTE commitment to extensive planting alongside the guided busway, including 145 new trees plus 2,000 hedges and other plants. West Midlands County Council engaged Halcrow Fox & Associates as consultants and Shand to construct the busway

itself, work being sufficiently advanced for the first test run to be made on 5 September 1984. At 22.00, with representatives from WMPTE and MCW on board, the testbed vehicle, MCW Metrobus 2686, in standard WMPTE livery of blue and cream, entered the 'to city' track and thus became the first guided bus to run in the UK and the world's first guided double-decker. The following night two-way

running was trialled, black-and-silver Metrobus 8107 being the first of the dedicated fleet of 14 vehicles to venture onto the busway.

The busway was substantially built, with steel guide rails on a concrete base as well as six 'stations' (inbound and outbound at each of three stops) where passengers had level access to the platform of the bus. At the entrance to each section of busway

# Developing Tracline 65

Martin Fisher, an engineer with WMPTE, was involved in the development of Tracline 65.

The track construction at MIRA and the track in Streetly Road were virtually identical, and in neither case was a German-style concrete trough used. The 'rails' were box-section, carried on right-angle 'chairs' on a concrete road surface; the only difference between MIRA and Streetly was that for the latter the space behind the rails was then back-filled, largely for appearance. The curves at intersections and crossings were cast in concrete, with no steel contact surface, and were of a much tighter radius than those used in Germany. (It was alleged that West Midlands County Council had inadvertently copied the German radii, forgetting they were measured in metres rather than feet, but I'm sure there was no truth in that …) This construction method was used mainly for speed and resulted in the exact opposite of the German layout, which used concrete running rails and steel blades at intersections and crossings.

It was often considered that the pronounced bump felt passing through gaps, which was far more noticeable than on the Essen system, was because of the sharper curves. While this may have been partially true, two other factors were found. One was that it was vital that the guide wheels lost contact with the rails at exactly the

same point; the difference of a few millimetres could result in the steering 'kicking', with no opportunity for the driver to rectify it before re-entering the guideway. However, I believe that the main reason, which was never proven, was that the cast-steel guide arms supplied by GKN were far more rigid than those used in the German systems, which were of a lighter, tubular design; although the overall free width of the guide wheels of 2,610mm within a track width of 2,600mm was the same, the force needed to 'squeeze' the wheels into the track was higher with the British design, resulting in the sharper kick. Without the 10mm interference the bus tended to yaw from side to side in an unpleasant manner, with the steering wheel vibrating; checking the overall width and re-shimming if necessary was one of the few additional tasks needed in maintaining the Tracline buses.

The German systems were developed under guidance from the Federal Ministry for Research and Technology, through research company SNV of Hamburg, which set the criteria for both Mercedes and MAN and, indirectly for the WM system also, as it was a state requirement that the standards should allow open access to all.

*Above:* A sweeping view along the Streetly Road guided busway. DAVID COLE

the trough sides were splayed out to 'funnel' the guided buses onto the track. This was not just at the start and finish but also at intermediate gaps in the reservation, as, despite the short overall length, it was felt that closing the reservation gaps would be a step too far.

Much play was made of the fact that the busway took up 25% less space than a conventional road for two-way bus operation. Technically, of course, it was just a bus lane, being part of the highway for which a Traffic Regulation Order had been obtained restricting access to guided buses. This left the responsibility for maintenance with the Highways Authority and not the PTE.

Elsewhere on route 65, bus stops were enhanced, information displays improved, waiting restrictions imposed (on the narrow sections of Slade Road) and some junctions improved to provide a more attractive service. South of Salford Circus ('Spaghetti Junction') these enhancements also benefited other routes which shared the same corridor into Birmingham city centre, although only buses on the 65 service were fitted with transponders that gave them a 'green wave' free run through traffic lights — not merely on the busway itself but also in Lichfield Road, Aston.

Following extensive trials the guided busway, now named Tracline, was formally

*Above:* A distinctive metal badge was issued to Tracline 65 drivers. DAVID COLE

*Left:* On opening day 8111 turns out of the Short Heath terminus on full lock, clearly showing the orange-painted guide-wheel assembly. DAVID COLE

*Left:* **Despite regular use on the guided busway 2686 retained the standard WMPTE livery of blue and cream. Here it has been turned out for a party of visitors in November 1984.**
**MARTIN FISHER**

opened on 9 October 1984 by James Isaacs, Director General of WMPTE, and Phil Bateman, Chairman of the county's Transportation Committee. There followed a short period of intensive free demonstration — probably the only occasion throughout its existence that more than one or two vehicles would be in view at the same time on the guided busway. Around noon normal service commenced, the black-and-silver guided Metrobuses replacing conventional vehicles and the public being directed to the new 'stations'.

The overall package was a success, apparently

# Operating Tracline 65

Geoff Kelland, a mobile inspector with WMPTE, was involved in the operation of Tracline 65.

The mobile inspector's first duty in the morning was to check the busway for obstructions, though it was on record that bricks placed in the guideway would be broken up by the vehicle rather than cause any problem; similarly, it was impossible to skid except in a straight line.

I believe that there were no grounds for safety fears, as there was only one incident involving guide wheels with which I was involved. There had been an incident on Slade Road near Salford Circus, and service 65 was diverted via Hillaries Road and Gravelly Hill in both directions. It was late-night service levels so probably a 20-minute headway. I was on late mobile duty and was asked to check out the diversionary route, which we did. On travelling up Hillaries Road we spotted a guide-wheel assembly lying in the road, having obviously come from a city-bound vehicle. Hillaries Road had no kerbs on the 'to city' side, only a grass bank, and the driver was unaware of what had happened. Because it was a time of low-frequency operation it was possible to identify the vehicle involved and get Miller Street to change the vehicle

before it arrived back on the busway.

At the start of a section of the guided busway the guide rails splayed out, with the offside being engaged first then the nearside, at which point the driver was relieved of the need to steer. It was soon found out that whilst in 'guide' mode the steering wheel should not be held but the hands should be placed flat on the top — the reason being that where a road junction was encountered the guide rails had a gap to allow other road users to cross, and if the steering wheel was held tightly and the bus wandered a sharp jolt was experienced when the guide rails were taken up again, which had caused injuries. In fact the trick to ensure as smooth a passage as possible across these gaps was to negotiate them as quickly as possible.

There were six passenger stations, as the bus shelters were known, which were reached by ramps giving stepless access to the bus platform, with an absolute minimum gap. Also tip-up seats were provided, and what we now know as real-time information was installed.

*Above:* Initial tests were carried out at MIRA, near Nuneaton, where on 30 April 1984 the press were given a demonstration of the system. No 8104 is seen being filmed as it joins the test track. **MARTIN FISHER**

*Above:* At one of the guided busway 'stations' 8113 shows the 'call help' facility available on the electronic destination display. **DAVID COLE**

swelling passenger numbers by more than 29% in the first year, at a time when overall bus use in the WMPTE area was growing at around 4%. Although almost identical other than in livery and the fitting of guide wheels, the black-and-silver buses were perceived by passengers as better — perhaps due partly to the drivers, who were specially trained for the route and wore distinctive badges for their role.

For nearly two years Tracline 65, operating at frequencies of up 4 minutes during peak hours, was a routine element of Birmingham's transport system. But on the horizon was deregulation. Would any other operator consider equipping its vehicles to compete on the busway? WMPTE's commercial successor, West Midlands Travel, apparently thought not and chose not to register a Sunday service on the route, probably confident that no one else would bid if the route were put out to tender. That the Sunday service was awarded to Midland Red West must therefore have come as a surprise but obviously made financial sense to the awarding body, WMPTE. Sunday passengers would henceforth need to use

the 'emergency' stops, without waiting shelters, on the conventional carriageways alongside the guided busway.

This may have been the visible beginning of the end, but another facet of deregulation, the need to cut unnecessary costs, was already exercising minds at West Midlands Travel. The premium paid to Tracline drivers fell into this category, and talks with the still strongly unionised workforce apparently failed to reach a satisfactory solution. Withdrawal of route 65 from the guided busway and the dispersal of the guided buses therefore made economic sense, and the last journeys along the guided busway ran on 27 September 1987. Thereafter standard vehicles, in blue and cream, took over, observing the stops already used on Sundays by Midland Red West.

The busway itself was eventually removed, and the reservation landscaped. Today, little remains to recall the operation. South of Salford Circus the route into the city centre was upgraded in 1998, when the partly parallel route 67 was converted to operation with articulated buses. The 65 still serves Short Heath, but the core service has not terminated

*Left:* **About to operate the last Tracline 65 guided-bus journey, Metrobus 8108 prepares to leave Short Heath on 27 September 1987. MARTIN FISHER**

there since deregulation and is normally operated by National Express West Midlands with low floor Scania single-deckers on a frequency of up to every eight minutes at peak hours. A local operator provides some competition with step-entrance Dennis Darts.

For many years the 'No Entry' sign guarding the turning bay at Short Heath retained 'except guided buses' as an exemption, whilst other artefacts were salvaged for Birmingham's Aston Manor Road Transport Museum. The most significant of these exhibits is one of the original guided Metrobuses, 8110, which in 2010 was restored to Tracline livery.

Technically, there is no reason to regard Tracline 65 as anything but a success. That it was built in the first place was a significant achievement at a time when metropolitan counties were about to be abolished and environmental issues such as the loss of trees were distracting politicians anxious to secure their future in the new political structure.

## The buses

The world's first guided double-deckers were the 15 MCW Metrobuses for the Birmingham guided busway, consisting of testbed 2686 (A686 UOE), which retained standard WMPTE colours, and the production batch of 14 — 8101-14 (A101-14 WVP) — in dedicated Tracline 65 livery. Mechanically they were standard vehicles with a cut-out in the skirting forward of the front wheels, for the guide arms. These latter were substantial steel assemblies with a guide wheel at the outer extremity, painted orange and given reflectors and indicator repeaters for enhanced visibility. The underframe was also strengthened with substantial steel plating to cope with the potential stresses generated by guided-busway operation.

The guide arms took the vehicles over the maximum width permitted by contemporary Construction & Use regulations, requiring special dispensation for their operation over the 65

*Left:* **Last of the former Tracline 65 Metrobuses to remain operational with Travel West Midlands was 2971 (originally 8111), seen turning from Navigation Street into Hill Street, above Birmingham's New Street station, in the summer of 2004. DAVID COLE**

*Right:* Metrobus 8110 freshly restored to Tracline 65 livery at Aston Manor Road Transport Museum in July 2010. DAVID COLE

*Left:* Today the Streetly Road reservation has reverted to nature, and buses on route 65 stop at modern shelters adjacent to the carriageway, as demonstrated by a National Express West Midlands Alexander-bodied Volvo B7TL. DAVID COLE

*Right:* One of the few reminders of the guided busway in the Streetly Road area is the 'except guided buses' exemption on the 'No Entry' sign at Short Heath. It is ignored every 10 minutes, as here by an outbound 65. DAVID COLE

*Left:* Opening day on the East Leeds busway included parallel pairing of Arriva and First double-deckers. Both buses are Volvo B7TLs with Alexander ALX400 bodywork. STUART JONES

route, emergency diversions and to their depot. The production Tracline vehicles differed from other Mk 2 Metrobuses in the WMPTE fleet by having the front numberplate mounted centrally (although this was often changed following accident repairs in later life).

In addition to testbed 2686, some of the production vehicles were used for driver training on a short length of development track at MIRA, the research establishment near Nuneaton. On 30 April 1984 the MIRA trials were shown to the press, also revealing the vehicles' black and silver Tracline scheme, designed by consultant George Kozlowski and apparently based on the colours of an American Football team. The impression of modernity was reinforced by Vultron Transdot electronic destination displays. On 8101-7 a separate number box was provided above a single line which displayed alternately the ultimate and intermediate destinations, while on 8108-14 the aperture was larger to provide the number box with two static lines continuously displaying the ultimate destination and 'via' points. The electronic displays, together with the guide arms and special livery, added £7,000 to the cost of a standard WMPTE Metrobus.

The production vehicles were used for special duties as well as driver training prior to the formal opening of the guided busway, most notably on hotel shuttle services for the Rotary International Convention at the National Exhibition Centre in the first week of June 1984, naturally without guide wheels fitted.

The Tracline 65 Metrobuses were based initially at Miller Street depot, at one time home to some of the trams which had operated to Short Heath. Miller Street closed operationally on 25 October 1986, in advance of deregulation, and for its final

months the service was worked from Hockley. With the cessation of Tracline 65 the guide arms were removed from the vehicles, and all but 8101 were quickly repainted into the standard West Midlands Travel livery of blue and cream. No 8101 initially remained silver, receiving the Timesaver branding designed for the dual-purpose Metrobuses delivered in 1986, before eventually gaining standard colours. Reflecting their conversion to standard vehicles, 8101-14 were renumbered 2961-74, following on from the dual-purpose batch.

During the 1990s the erstwhile Tracline 65 fleet was dispersed, standard destination equipment installed and the later silver-and-blue livery applied. With the exception of 2964, lost in an arson attack at Hockley depot in July 1994, all were included in the extensive refurbishment programme undertaken (mainly by Marshall of Cambridge) in the mid-1990s, enabling their continued service into the new millennium. Refurbishment included a revised rear-end design and removal of the strengthening plates installed for guided-busway operation.

The rapid influx from 2000 of new low-floor double-deckers rendered many Metrobuses redundant, although there was a strong second-hand market, and 10 of the Tracline 65 fleet readily found new owners. By their 21st birthday in early 2005 three remained with Travel West Midlands — 2970 and 2974 at Coventry, complete with sky-blue relief and Travel Coventry fleetnames, and 2971 at West Bromwich, recently repainted with red relief. When their operation at Coventry ended, 2970 was chosen for preservation at Aston Manor, while 2974 attracted the day's highest bids when sold in the May 2005 Miller Street auction to McColls of Balloch. No 2971 continued in service for several more months before being the only normal withdrawal to make a direct trip to the scrapyard. Some vehicles were to have long lives with their new owners, 2961 (8101) being still in use with Travel de Courcey in 2011.

### The next generation in the UK

Following termination of Tracline 65 seven years would elapse before guided buses returned to the UK, with the opening in Ipswich of a short section of guided busway giving a priority route to specially equipped Dennis Darts operated by Eastern Counties. This operation continues under First, although the busway has required modification to accommodate the increased width of more modern vehicles.

The UK's most significant commitment to guided operation has been in West Yorkshire, where three heavily used corridors have been equipped with stretches of segregated busway. Scott Hall Road in Leeds was followed by the impressive continuous central reservation guided busway in York Road, also in Leeds, and the Manchester Road scheme in Bradford, noted for its futuristic passenger shelters. The latter schemes reintroduced guided double-deckers and from the start involved two operators — First and Arriva.

Short stretches of strategic guided busway have also been installed in Crawley as part of the town's Fastway scheme, operated by Metrobus with Scania single-deckers. In Scotland, a reserved track was constructed in Edinburgh's western suburbs and operated initially as a guided busway prior to conversion to planned light-rail operation.

In recent years guided busways have been promoted as a more flexible alternative to the reinstatement of closed railways. Schemes for Cambridge-St Ives, Gosport and Luton-Dunstable have taken priority, construction commencing first on the Cambridge project for an initial projected opening date in late 2009. This project has, however, been beset with constructional and contractual issues that have introduced a series of delays to the route's opening, which finally took place in August 2011. In the meantime both participating operators, Stagecoach and Go Whippet, had to waiting to make full use of their appropriately equipped low-floor, low-emission vehicles, procured in readiness for the initial start date.

### European developments

Guided buses have featured in the development plans of several European cities, again with mixed success. Mannheim, home of Mercedes-Benz bus production, overlaid conventional guided-busway facilities on an existing tram reservation and ran guide-wheel-equipped buses for almost two decades. In France, alternative approaches have been tried, blurring the boundaries between guided bus, trolleybus and light rail with pneumatic-tyred vehicles guided by a single central rail or optically through specialised road markings.

Alternative guidance systems have also been considered for the UK. As early as 1974 the Transport & Road Research Laboratory experimented with electronic control using a Daimler Roadliner, and in 1996 an experimental installation was demonstrated in Newcastle using AEG systems and an Optare Prisma-bodied Mercedes-Benz O.405.

**Martin Fisher, an engineer with WMPTE, was involved in the development of Tracline 65.**

*Left:* **One of the French approaches to guided buses, the Bombardier trolleybus system installed in Caen features a single steel rail for guidance and current-return purposes. The vehicles have a limited off-track capability with normal steering. The system opened in 2002. DAVID COLE**

# Going green in the Lakes

Open-top buses are not found only at the seaside. **Tony Wilson** illustrates a selection of those that have served the Lake District.

One usually associates open-top buses with the seaside, but for many years such vehicles have served the land-locked waters of Cumbria, where during the summer months the environs of Grasmere, Rydal Water and Windermere in the Central Lakes area, along with Derwent Water in the Northern Lakes, have been served by a variety of roofless vehicles.

From around Easter to September the main roads between the village of Grasmere and the landing stage at Bowness-on-Windermere have been regularly served by what is nowadays route 599. Further north another service operates from the main town of Keswick through Borrowdale to the foot of the Honister Pass at Seatoller. As is often the case, buses that had served for many years in front-line service were converted for open-top service — although one must not forget that over the years a number of buses have built as convertible open-toppers.

The Lake District is designated as an Area of Outstanding Natural Beauty, and, perhaps with this in mind, many of the buses operating around the Central Lakes were for a number of years painted in a pseudo-Southdown green livery that harmonised with the landscape.

*Below:* **The Guide Friday company was established in the mid-1980s at Stratford-upon-Avon, in Warwickshire. By the end of the decade it had expanded to other parts of the UK and set up an operation in the Lake District. Here its service ran every 20 minutes between Bowness and Ambleside alongside the eastern shores of Windermere. One of the regular buses was this former Midland Red Alexander-bodied Fleetline, which had been new in 1969. It is seen near Windermere railway station.**

*Above:* By 1990 the service was in the hands of the Stagecoach's Cumberland subsidiary. With a distinctive livery derived from that of Southdown, taken over by Stagecoach the previous year, the service was marketed as the Lakeland Experience. Among the vehicles employed was this former Devon General Leyland Atlantean bodied by Metro-Cammell as a convertible open-topper, pictured turning onto the landing stage at Bowness-on-Windermere on a busy day in July.

*Below:* Operated alongside the Atlantean were several Bristol VRTs. These too had been built as convertible open-toppers and delivered in 1978 to Southdown. Their employment on the South Coast concluded, a small number migrated north within the Stagecoach group, this one being seen at the entrance to Windermere station.

*Left:* **By May 1995 the service had been extended northwards from the Ambleside terminus past Rydal Water to the village of Grasmere. Far away from its original home was this 1966 Metro-Cammell-bodied Leyland Atlantean, whose early days were spent serving the inhabitants of Portsmouth and Southsea in the ownership of Portsmouth Corporation.**

*Right:* **Another ex-Southdown VRT in Keswick, heading for Seatoller, in 1998. Note the blue bike logos on the front.**

*Left:* **A rear view of the same bus reversing at the Seatoller terminus, showing the bike rack. The route takes in the entire length of Borrowdale.**

*Left:* In what many would regard as typical Lake District weather, an ex-Ribble ECW-bodied Leyland Olympian arrives at Windermere station in 2002.

*Right:* The open-top Olympians operated alongside Leyland Titans formerly operated by Stagecoach's East London subsidiary. After 18 years serving the capital a Titan enjoys a quieter life operating on the Lakeland Experience in May 2002. The location is Grasmere.

*Left:* In September 2007 there were still open-top Titans in the Lake District, but now in corporate Stagecoach colours, rather than genteel green and cream, and with Lakes Rider branding. This 23-year-old Titan is approaching the southern terminus of the route at Bowness-on-Windermere.

*Above:* By 2009 the Lake District open-toppers were again green, albeit applied in corporate style, and the step-entrance Titans had been replaced by low-floor Dennis Tridents with Alexander ALX400 bodywork. Like the Titans, the Tridents started life as dual-door buses operating in London. A short roof section provides shelter for passengers in the forward rows.

*Below:* In 2010 the Borrowdale service was worked by two Alexander-bodied Leyland Olympians. Here the pair meet at the mid-point of the route between Keswick and Seatoller.

# Taking the bus for a walk

**Les Dickinson** looks back 50 years to Peak District hikes and some of the unusual buses that served his home city of Sheffield.

*All photographs from the author's collection*

I am Sheffield-born and bred, but my work has taken me into many other operators' territories. Sheffield Transport Department and Sheffield Joint Omnibus Committee have always held top spot in my league of operators. As a teenager in the 1960s I spent many hours on the study of the Sheffield fleet. I was able to identify almost every vehicle from the Leadmill Road garage by the varying combination of adverts carried by each and the subtle variations in livery application. My knowledge at that time was such that it would have been a fairly safe specialist subject with which to enter Mastermind.

It is this background which drives me to write about some of Sheffield's unique vehicles, which added to the allure of this never-dull fleet.

First, a comment on the livery. I have seen this described as 'seriously impractical'. To me this livery was head and shoulders above all others (Me? Biased? Surely not?), and despite some very difficult operating conditions in this once heavily industrial city — and especially in those dirty winter months of rain, snow and slush — every vehicle emerged from its garage ready for duty looking quite resplendent. The evidence is there in the photographs. These buses brought a bit of light into this busy city.

There are many other liveries which have met with my approval along the way, including the chocolate, biscuit and cream worn formerly by East Midland and the smart blues of The Delaine. I found a little strange the misguided adventure by Sheffield into a horrible all-over green livery. This thankfully short-lived experiment was reportedly much derided by the good folk of Sheffield, as was the awful livery adopted some years later by South Yorkshire PTE. That's another story worth a few pages in its own right … or perhaps not; it was so dire it's probably best to make no further comment.

Whatever the livery, let me get on to my main reason for putting pen to paper — the tremendous variety of manufacturers favoured by Sheffield for chassis and bodywork. Several combinations have been unique. Prime examples were the five ECW-bodied Leyland Titan PD2/20s — 1152/3 (YWB 152/3) in the railway-owned 'C' fleet and 1292-4 (YWB 292-4) in the 'B' fleet, owned jointly by Sheffield Corporation and British Railways. These were great vehicles but, for me, were overshadowed

*Right:* Among the unusual vehicles in the Sheffield fleet were five Leyland Titans with highbridge ECW bodywork of a style more commonly found on Bristol chassis. One is seen in Leeds bus station.

*Left:* Even more unusual were a pair of Titans with bodywork by Mann Egerton of Norwich, which operated in Sheffield from 1952 to 1965. Alongside in this view stand a Weymann-bodied Titan of 1957 and an AEC Regent III, also bodied by Weymann and dating from 1947.

by two other Titans, 361/2 (NWE 561/2), which had rare double-deck Mann Egerton bodies built in 1952. Going back to 1294, this was regularly used on my home route, the 83 to Birley, which was then a little way outside the city boundary; because of this the return journey would always show 'Sheffield' rather than 'City'.

I often had the pleasure of using the single-deck ECWs as well. Coach-bodied 1180-82 (1880-2 WA) of the 'C' fleet and 1310/1 (1910/1 WA) of the 'B' fleet would regularly take me into Derbyshire's Peak District for my weekend hiking expeditions. All were based on Leyland Leopard L1 chassis, this being another combination exclusive to Sheffield. My jaunts took me to places such as Buxton, Tideswell, Great Hucklow (where hours could be spent watching the gliders soar over miles of open

countryside) and Eyam, where brave villagers had confined themselves during the Great Plague to prevent it from spreading any further.

On hike days we would ride out on one of the well-appointed ECW coaches and back to town at the end of the day on a Weymann Fanfare, or maybe a dual-purpose Burlingham. The Fanfares were 1170-74 (6170-4 WJ), 1300-5 (1500-5 WJ), and 1312-14 (1912-4 WA). The Burlinghams were 1175-9 (5875-9 W) and 1306-9 (5906-9 W). Each of these was a treat to ride and quite special in what was in essence a municipal fleet. As each was mounted on a Leopard L1 chassis perhaps the title of this story should have been 'Taking the cat for a walk'. On rare occasions the sole AEC Reliance coach, 900 (9000 WB), with 37-seat centre-entrance Roe Dalesman body, was

*Left:* Besides the ECW-bodied Titans Sheffield ran equally unusual ECW-bodied Leyland Leopards. There were five, new in 1961.

*Above:* From an earlier generation of Sheffield single-decker was this 1948 AEC Regal with 34-seat rear-entrance Weymann body, seen on layover in the city after a trip to Bakewell.

*Below:* More unusual rear-entrance single-deckers were two Weymann-bodied Leyland Royal Tigers delivered in 1953. They were normally to be found on the 31 service to Upperthorpe.

to be seen in Derbyshire, even though this was an 'A'-fleet vehicle, owned wholly by the Corporation. In the Sheffield fleet the centre entrance was itself a novelty. The coach was essentially a plaything for council committees and seldom saw any real work.

The Peak District journeys were a real treat for anyone interested in bus travel. As well as the great variety of Sheffield buses there were other operators to see en route. I recall on arrival at the Fox House Inn, at Longshaw, seeing a Chesterfield Corporation all-Crossley single-decker. Now, if you were going to have a green livery then Chesterfield's rich dark green with cream relief was the only way to go! Fox House was a meeting of the ways. Three of Sheffield's routes stopped there before taking their various tracks. During the summer months many duplicates would operate short runs terminating here, often using 'deckers from all three parts of the fleet. Many a shandy has been supped inside and outside the hostelry whilst awaiting connections or waiting to meet fellow hikers arriving on a different bus.

Another, smaller operator sometimes seen whilst on these trips was Silver Service, which in the 1960s had some ageing but interesting half-cab single-deckers. The associated fleet of Hulleys was also a haven of mostly second-hand vehicles. Both were likely to be seen at Bakewell, another of my regular hiking haunts. Bakewell was always special and was the source of much extra revenue for SJOC, especially on bank-holiday weekends, when literally hundreds of Sheffielders would travel by bus to the Bakewell Show. On such occasions vehicles from all three fleets would be seen, along with visiting coaches.

On bank holidays there would be a seemingly endless convoy of double-deckers — Regents and Titans galore, exposed radiators and tin fronts. In my earlier years all the double-deckers were 27ft long, although latterly they were augmented by 30-footers to maximise revenue more cost-effectively. With the passage of time these in turn were replaced by Atlanteans and Fleetlines, and in SYPTE days, Dennis Dominators.

Back to the heady days of Regent IIIs and Vs, and there was further excitement in the variety of coachbuilders that could sometimes be seen in Bakewell. These included Roberts, Northern Coachbuilders, Strachans, Cravens and, most common of all, Leyland, Roe and Weymann.

Back in town, I often used the 31 to Upperthorpe to visit relatives in the area. On my visits there was seldom any variety, and the service was always operated by single-deckers. However, among the regulars were 222/3 (RWA 222/3), which, if not

*Below:* **Weymann Fanfare coach bodies were relatively uncommon. Sheffield had 11 on Leyland Leopard L1 chassis.**

*Left:* Illustrating Sheffield Transport's reach out to the surrounding countryside is this view of a Burlingham-bodied Leopard, loading in Buxton for a trip back to the city soon after delivery in 1960.

unique in England, were certainly unusual. They were Royal Tigers with Weymann bodywork, the rarity lying in the cut-away rear entrance with high steps, the use of which almost qualified as an 'extreme sport'. I never ever witnessed these two on any other route. Other buses that were sometimes used on the 31 included four Leyland/MCW Olympics (including one ex-demonstrator), four Leopards and three AEC Regal IVs.

Another significant batch of unusual buses comprised 20 Alexander-bodied AEC Regent V 2D3RAs, delivered in 1960 together with 26 Weymann- and 25 Roe-bodied examples. The attractive Alexander design was easily distinguishable by the domed roof. Alexander bodies of this type were not common in England, and when East Midland received some Albion Lowlanders they were instantly identifiable as Alexander products, because of those domes. The only other Alexander double-decker in the Sheffield fleet at the time was 369 (1369 W), a Leyland Atlantean PDR1/1 which I thought quite ugly and

ill-proportioned. How could the same builder produce the beauties that were the Regents and the beast that was the Atlantean?

Another one-off in the fleet was the seemingly enormous 'box on wheels', the forward-entrance AEC Bridgemaster, 525 (1925 WA). It is great to see this bus preserved to such a high standard; it gladdens the heart. This, together with the five rear-entrance examples, spent much of its working life on the Gleadless routes. Like Rome, Sheffield is built on seven hills. This is arduous territory, and the long drag up East Bank Road many times a day with several stops seriously tested these workhorses. No doubt the hill starts, fully laden, will have tested the resolve of many a driver too.

In later years Sheffield was served by unusual vehicles in PTE ownership, including a unique East Lancs-bodied Foden, an Atlantean — and rather more Ailsas — with Van Hool McArdle bodywork, Leyland-DAB artics and Dennis Dominos. But the oddities of 50 years ago retain a special appeal.

*Left:* Among the Sheffield types that appealed to the author were the 20 Alexander-bodied AEC Regent Vs delivered in 1960. They were 30ft-long 69-seaters and had the only bodies of this style to be supplied to an English operator.

# The longest day

At the start of 2011 **Stewart J. Brown** made his longest-ever bus trip. Here he tells the tale.

*All photographs by the author*

I knew it was going to be a long journey, but hadn't realised quite how long when we climbed aboard the bus in San Felix bus station. It was only as we were leaving the edge of the town, where a road sign listed destinations and distances, that I became aware that I was embarking on my longest-ever bus trip. At the bottom of the list was our destination: Santa Elena, 717 kilometres. Add the distance we had already covered, and we were looking at a trip of almost 450 miles. It was a family visit, to one of my wife's cousins, who lives in the south of Venezuela, close to the border with Brazil. Her cousins live in exotic places — Santa Elena, Caracas, Buenos Aires. Mine live in Hamilton, Dumfries and Orpington. No competition.

We'd actually started our trip the previous morning in Puerto Ordaz, just a few miles north of San Felix. We'd been at Puerto Ordaz bus station at 7am, hoping to catch an 8.30 coach to Santa Elena. There was, it appears, no such coach. There would be a coach at some later, unspecified time that morning. Or maybe not. If there were no passengers wanting to alight in Puerto Ordaz the coach might just bypass the town. But, we were assured, there were plenty of buses running between San Felix and Santa Elena.

If this all seems a bit vague, that's because it was. Some companies have websites, but not all. And I've yet to find any Venezuelan website — even for internationally recognised car-hire companies — where you can book or pay online. Bus timetables are hard to come by. On the services we used the tickets were written by hand, as were booking charts. I felt the clock had been turned back.

A Volvo with double-deck Marcopolo coach body was in one of the bays in Puerto Ordaz bus station. Yes, the driver said, he was going to San Felix. We boarded via the centre door, sat on the upper deck and made our way — unchallenged and free of charge — to San Felix. So far, so good. But *plenty* of buses to Santa Elena? Hmmm. There was an 8.15, but it was full. The clerk in the bus company's office said the next day's bus was full too, but we could have seats on the bus on the day after.

We considered our options, while watching the bus station's wildlife — mangy dogs wandering listlessly, mosquitoes and, the star of the show, a large rat scuttling across the roof beams. As my old granny used to say, we may not be rich, but we do see life. We could get a ticket to a town imaginatively named Kilometre 88, but that would leave us in the middle of nowhere, with no guarantee of an onward

*Left:* **The Encava-bodied Isuzu refuels on its 450-mile trip from San Felix to Santa Elena.**

connection. (And when we later passed through Kilometre 88 we were glad not to be stopping.) We could travel on an overnight coach. Now, I don't know when or how I will die, but I have this sense that overnight travel on a South American coach shortens the odds on dying sooner rather than later. So that option was ruled out.

Another chat with the bus company's clerk revealed that she thought the company might run an extra bus the next day. If we phoned her at 6.30 on the following morning she'd let us know. So we decided to spend the day in San Felix, quickly realising that the bus station was in fact one of the high-points of the town. The accommodation which was available can best be described as interesting. There is no San Felix Hilton. Not even a San Felix Travelodge. I quickly realised that Coatbridge was not the worst town in the universe. San Felix is much, much worse.

The following morning couldn't come quickly enough, and at 6.30 we called the clerk. There was to be no extra bus … *but* … two passengers had cancelled on the 8am departure, so we could have their seats. Success at last. Most of the vehicles running in and out of San Felix bus station were moderately respectable, among them luxurious high-floor Volvos and a fair number of B12R-based tri-axle double-deck coaches.

We weren't to be quite so fortunate.

Our transport was based on an Isuzu 9-tonne truck chassis, bodied by Venezuelan builder Encava, and operated by a company called Turgar. Encava is big in midi-sized vehicles, producing the same basic body as a two-door bus or, as in this case, a single-door 35-seat coach. Think of it as a Bedford SB for the 21st century, about 9m long and 2.2m

wide. It had reclining seats, but the retaining springs had long since failed. It had generous leg room. It had air-conditioning — but that didn't work, so ventilation was provided by keeping the sliding windows open for most of the trip. And it was remarkably comfortable. The ride was smooth. I have very grave reservations about Venezuelans' driving abilities, but the driver was first-class.

Once we were all on board, the conductor announced the coach would not be stopping, so if anybody wanted to go to the toilet they should do so now. Half of the passengers then got off again to avail themselves of the bus station's facilities. This, however, was a Venezuelan conductor's joke: we made two stops at roadside restaurants on our trip. We also stopped twice for diesel and four times at military checkpoints, which are a feature of Venezuela's roads. At the last the soldier didn't just check our identity documents but checked our luggage too — meaning we all had to get out the bus, retrieve our cases and have them inspected. They're on the look-out for drugs. Santa Elena is just 10 miles from the Brazilian border, and Venezuela takes a tough line on drug transporters.

The service picked up and set down a few passengers along the way. At its busiest I counted 40, with three sitting on the engine cover and two on the conductor's seat, opposite the driver. There were in fact 41 — I'd missed a lady sitting in the stairwell. The coach version of the Encava body has a plug door which may once have been power-operated. On this coach it was secured in the closed position by a length of rope tied around a stanchion supporting the bulkhead behind the driver.

The road from San Felix to Santa Elena is good — think A-road Britain — with long straight

stretches across the flatlands and impossibly steep curving sections through the mountains, which reduced the Isuzu to little more than walking pace on some of the most severe gradients.

Having left just after 8am, we reached Santa Elena at 7pm — an 11-hour journey with one driver and two breaks of around 30 minutes.

Arranging our return trip was challenging. There seemed to be four companies offering through services to Puerto Ordaz, with their own offices in the bus station. And the concept of customer-care training was clearly alien. In one office the clerk declined to open the door, preferring to shuffle papers. In another the response could be summarised as: Can't you see I'm too busy to worry about tickets for travel next week? Go away! But the bus station — sorry, the international passenger terminal — was actually

*Above:* **Many Encava buses have two doors. Here the conductor supervises as schoolgirls board a bus bound for Ciudad Guayana, another name used for Puerto Ordaz and its satellite towns.**

quite nice and clean, albeit not over busy.

There were three daytime departures from Santa Elena to Puerto Ordaz, at 11am, noon and 1pm. We finally — on the morning of travel — got tickets for the noon departure operated by a Brazilian company, Eucatur. Now this was a through service which was making a 36-hour trip from Manaus in Brazil to Puerto La Cruz, on the Venezuelan coast (a distance I reckon to be around 1,400 miles), and I wasn't entirely confident it would appear on time. But it did. Mind you, by the time some passengers had got off and others had got on and

*Right:* **The Eucatur Volvo B10M pauses for a meal break on the 11-hour trip from Santa Elena to Puerto Ordaz. The functionality of the headlights — clearly working here — would later be the subject of discussion and the cause of delay.**

luggage had been dealt with it was 12.25pm before we left. Forget the traffic commissioners' window of tolerance on departure times. By Venezuelan standards that counts as on-time performance.

The coach was a three-axle Volvo B10M with high-floor 44-seat Marcopolo body — near enough 4m high to judge by the double-decker standing alongside. As on many South American coaches, there was a full-width bulkhead, with a centrally located door, behind the entrance area, effectively sealing the driver off in his own compartment. This was travelling business class, compared with the Isuzu's economy class, although on some sections of the route the air suspension caused the coach to yaw, like a boat on a sea with a mild swell. It was fitted with seat belts, with a notice on the seat back warning that their use was *obrigatorio*, and quoting the relevant legislation — although I suspect this particular law was treated with no more respect in Brazil than it was in Venezuela.

The army checks were slower. Firstly, there were more people. Secondly, most of them were Brazilians, whose passports needed to be checked. On the southbound Isuzu I had been the only foreigner. There was one meal stop, and one fuel stop. Then came the delay. It was dark, and at one of the checkpoints there was some discussion about the adequacy of the coach's headlights. The upshot was that after an hour at the roadside we were escorted by a police car to the next checkpoint. The

police car led — presumably lighting the way ahead — and whatever the concerns were it didn't slow us down, as we passed slower vehicles on the road. At the next checkpoint the police car turned back, and we continued on our way. Curious. Being of a suspicious nature I assumed some sort of police scam — but fear I'll never know.

After dark there was no interior lighting in the coach, except when stopped at checkpoints. No reading lights, no emergency night lights, and certainly no fancy gangway lights. This meant that it was pitch dark, except for the odd glow when somebody switched on a mobile phone. It's an odd feeling travelling through dark country, in a dark coach, literally — and I don't exaggerate — unable to see your hand in front of your face.

Even with the one-hour delay the return trip still took 11 hours, this no doubt reflecting the superior performance of the Volvo over the little Isuzu.

The trips did not mark the extremes of Venezuelan bus travel. I doubt if there are any coaches more luxurious than the Volvo, which is representative of vehicles used on express services throughout the country — although mostly operated by Venezuelan companies. But at

the other extreme there are services operated by what are in effect US school buses — often very colourful — and by elderly Mercedes-Benz O.302 integrals dating from the 1970s.

And British-built buses? The last of 450 Leyland Nationals supplied to Caracas in the 1970s came out of service in 2007 — quite a remarkable performance, considering that many of these over-sophisticated buses saw only four or five years in service. And the other remarkable survivor, also in 2007, was a Commer minibus operating a local service in Sanare, a town in the mountains in the west of the country.

*Above:* This Blue Bird coach is nearing the 4,118m summit of the road across Pico del Aguila (Eagle's Peak), the highest road in Venezuela. The winding road can be seen in the background. That the coach is on the wrong side of the road is not a matter of great concern (except, perhaps, to the passengers).

*Left:* A US-built Ford on the long climb to Sanare. The wording on the windscreen reads 'Special edition' and 'The best of the world'. The yellow on the headlight lenses are painted images of the stylised head of a fox.

*Above:* One British bus was running in Sanare as recently as 2007 — this Commer, which must have been around 40 years old.

*Below:* Britain's biggest bus success in Venezuela was the supply of 450 Nationals to Caracas. The National was too sophisticated for the city's operating environment, and most had very short lives. But a couple survived until 2007, when they and other older types were replaced by smart new Volvo B7RLEs.

# Just coasting along

**Chris Drew** presents images from places close to the coast around the British Isles.

It's Wednesday 27 October 2010, and I'm sitting on a beach near Southwold, in Suffolk. A merlin has just arrived on the final leg of its migration from Norway. Not flying full-tilt, more laid back, just coasting.

In the UK we're lucky in the many and varied ways that the land meets the sea. Towns sprang up where the going was easy, whilst elsewhere areas of high cliff, downland or boggy places made life harder. Where I'm sitting now is quite flat, easy to get a boat into. But the rocks are soft, and the full force of wind and tide have etched away at the foundations until whole villages have fallen under the waves.

It makes you think … if we carry on the way we are, maybe someone, not unlike myself, will at some future date be sitting on a beach just outside Birmingham watching a merlin end its journey, possibly viewing the scene from an open-topper on the Inner Circle service.

**Under operatic skies**

Aldeburgh, meaning 'Old Fort' (long lost to the sea), was a flourishing shipbuilding port. Drake's Golden Hind was laid down there, one of many ships to be launched from Aldeburgh's slipways. This was all lost as the River Alde began to silt up. Marshes formed, and today these are good areas to watch for such birds as curlew and hen harrier. The only boats around now are the small fishing vessels that get hauled out onto the beach. Bus services in the area are operated mainly by First or, as in this photograph, Anglian. A Mercedes-Benz Vario is seen heading towards Leiston along the narrow road across the marshy area behind the beach strand, with Aldeburgh silhouetted against the last of the sun's rays. The Mercedes, with Plaxton Beaver 2 body, started its journey in Ipswich.

## Where are we today?

What day is it? If it's Tuesday then Berwick must be in England. Slight exaggeration, but the town has been claimed by both sides of the border on several occasions. In the Middle Ages it popped backwards and forwards between the English and Scots like a shuttlecock. Geographically, the River Tweed would have made a very satisfactory border line. For a time the local bus operators, United Auto and Eastern Scottish, demonstrated Anglo-Scottish reconciliation by having their garages right next to each other and working out of the same bus station. Here an Eastern Scottish Alexander-bodied Bedford VAM — a very rare combination — pulls out of the aforementioned bus station on a late-evening journey to St Abbs, whom those who work out might consider the patron saint of muscles …

## Scotch mist

From the Falls of Measach, the A832 makes its way through the Dundonnell Forest. The clouds begin to close in over the peaks of An Teallach, and through Camusnagaul the leaden sky seems to be getting lower. Then, round the corner and coming at great speed, a Scottish Citylink coach heads for Inverness. Just as soon, it was gone, and it wasn't until I developed the film that I knew what I had taken — a Berkhof-bodied Dennis Javelin belonging to Rapson's.

## Island Titan

This is Balley Chashtal — or, in English, Castletown — on the Isle of Man. This town of narrow streets can be found on the north-west side of Castletown Bay, at the very south-eastern corner of the island. It was once the capital of the island and was the site of Tynwald, the oldest parliament in the world. It's still used as a productive fishing harbour, and holidaymakers flock there every year, many to see the basking sharks that come to feed in the summer months. Like many islands, it is a great pleasure to travel round, especially as on this visit in the 1960s most of the transport was provided by Leyland Titans — either PD3s or all-Leyland PD2s like this one, caught passing through on its way from Douglas to Port St Mary.

## A distant shore...

Its critics have been known to call it Weston-Super-Mud because of the great expanse of sand that is exposed at low tide, when the water's edge can be over a mile away from the promenade. Like many seaside towns of today, Weston was a small fishing village until the end of the 18th century, when it was 'discovered'. The railway arrived in 1841, and soon afterwards the Victorians began to leave their mark. Here in the early 1980s a former King Alfred Leyland Atlantean, converted to open-top, waits in the background as a Roe-bodied Olympian departs for Bristol. Both buses were operated by the Bristol Omnibus Co.

## ... and a distant island

This is Alderney. St Anne is the island's only town and has something of the air of Normandy about it — not surprising, because it's only eight miles from the French coast. In the middle of St Anne is Marais Square, where this cattle trough acts as a meeting-place and bus station, served by the small fleet of blue-and-white buses operated by Riduna Buses, which included this smart Leyland Tiger Cub with Saunders-Roe body.

### It's not all trams

For the best part of 40 years the principal focus of transport interest in Seaton, Devon, has been the narrow-gauge Seaton Tramway. The line is not only a great tourist attraction but also lays on specialist events such as learn-to-drive-a-tram lessons, vintage rallies and bird-watching trips from the trams — and I can vouch from personal experience that watching a hen harrier from a tram is slightly surreal but well worth it. And in the 1980s there were little buses like this Axe Valley Volkswagen LT working the afternoon X99 service to Rousdon.

### Pett Level

Between Hastings and Hythe lies a large, flat flood plain. In Saxon times the sea penetrated much further inland, reaching Winchelsea, Rye and the Romney Marshes, but over the years nature, with some help from man, has pushed the sea back to its present position. Here on Pett Level an East Kent AEC Reliance makes its way to Camber. A Mini, a Rover 2000 and a Commer caravanette complete this 1960s scene.

# The exoticism of the single-decker

Brought up in a double-deck world, **Michael H. C. Baker** reflects on how strange the world of single-deckers appeared to him.

I've never quite got used to riding single-deckers. This stems from the fact that I grew up in a double-deck world and still believe that a bus with stairs leading to a panoramic view over hedges and into other people's upstairs front rooms is every UK citizen's unalienable right. Indeed it has taken me something like half a century to become accustomed to the notion that an open platform at the back is not the only means of entering and alighting to and from the aforementioned double-decker.

Which is not to say I am advocating a return to smoke-filled upper decks, to the days when conductors had degrees in Cockney rhyming slang, when children of 18 months were shoved up chimneys, when no-one ever locked their front doors and we all adored being blown up by Dorniers and couldn't wait for the days when preserved steam railways would re-enact such jolly times.

But the fact is that my daily travels to school, or at weekends for pleasure (School not a pleasure? Well, perhaps …), were invariably in double-deckers, whether motor buses, trams or trolleybuses, and when one of the aforementioned Dorniers inconsiderately made our house uninhabitable and we took ourselves off to the Sussex coast, Southdown still provided double-deckers, beautiful green-and-cream Titans. Later, when dear Adolf had a second go at 8 Broughton Road with one of his 'doodlebugs' and only just missed, I then had the opportunity to go to school on a bright-yellow double-deck trolleybus and visit relations in a Hants & Dorset Titan. These latter (the Titans, not the relations), although certainly double-deckers, were of a variety I had never previously come across, having a trough-like gangway upstairs giving access to rows of seats, each with accommodation for four customers and ample opportunity for trampling on said customers' feet.

Just what was a coach and what was a single-deck bus was not always particularly distinct. In the 1920s there was the canvas-roofed charabanc

with rows of seats, each row with individual doors, which was essentially for a day trip to the country or seaside, quite different from the bus, but with the arrival at the end of that decade of the Leyland Tiger and the AEC Regal came the basis for a far more sophisticated vehicle which could bodied as either a bus or a coach. The bodywork which some builders provided for the former were little less luxurious than those for the latter, and at peak holiday times and weekends they were frequently called on to perform long-distance duties. There were 82 million coach journeys in 1936/7 as Britain slowly recovered from the Depression. Ribble acquired a large fleet of Leyland Tiger and Cheetah buses, which could regularly be seen at Blackpool and elsewhere on coach duties, and East Kent actually painted some of its Dennis Lancet buses into coach livery. Southdown's 1400-series Leyland TS7 and TS8 Tigers — particularly handsome vehicles — were another case in point.

The first journey I can recall making in a single-decker was in one of these Southdown Tigers, in 1941. It had been adapted to cope with wartime needs, and, although as handsome as ever externally, internally it could certainly not be described as luxurious. The seats were arranged all around the edges with a large space in the middle for standees, so that its capacity was nearly as great as that of a double-decker. This was on a trip to Horsham, a town where single-deckers were very much part of the scene — not only Southdown examples but others from London Transport and Aldershot & District. I never got to travel on one of the latter's; the only time I spent in the company's territory was during National Service in the RAF, when I was sent down from my regular posting at Abingdon — where we trained the Parachute Regiment to jump out of aeroplanes, rather than have to do something so stupidly dangerous ourselves — to spend a week at Aldershot, 'Home of the British Army'. In comparison with the Army the RAF was a bit of

*Right:* There was a degree of operational interchangeability between buses and coaches, as demonstrated by this Yorkshire Woollen Leyland Tiger PS1 with 34-seat bus bodywork, by Brush, at Blackpool on coach duties at the start of the 1950s.

a doddle, we lads in grey seldom being asked to march anywhere once basic training was over, whilst the Army seemed to take a masochistic delight in doing practically everything by numbers. Thus I did not care over much for Aldershot and by association Aldershot & District buses — very unfair on the buses, but there it was. Looking back I realise what attractive buses the company's half-cab Dennis single-deckers, in particular, were.

The nearest single-deckers to home in Croydon were the Green Line 10T10 AEC Regals, which actually passed the top of our road once Green Line services recommenced with the ending of the war. Excellent, indeed iconic vehicles they may have been, but by the standards of Southdown, whose Harrington-bodied Tigers passed the bottom of our road and really were coaches, Green Line vehicles were no more than glorified buses. The only single-

deck buses allocated to our local (Croydon) garage were six-wheel LTs — AEC Renowns dating from 1930/1 — for the 234 and 234A services. Sometime around 1948 I sampled a journey on the 234, an outer-suburban route, which ran from Riddlesdown (although officially Old Lodge Lane, Purley) out into the country, down the hill to the main A22/23 at Purley proper, then back up the North Downs past the charmingly named Smitham Bottom Lane to Wallington. I had the bus to myself at the start of the 23-minute journey and spread out on the long offside longitudinal seat peering into the far distance, where I could just make out the conductor standing by the entrance. It was probably as well that I did not realize that, to quote Ken Blacker, 'uncluttered by stanchions … there was nothing to support the [18-year-old] roof'. Subsequently double-decked, the 234 would later be worked by,

*Right:* An unusual view of a 1937 Leyland Tiger in the Southdown fleet, showing the comprehensive rear destination display. The body was by Harrington.

*Left:* One route local to the author when he lived in Croydon was operated by single-deckers, the 234. This is an AEC Renown.

amongst others, the unique front-entrance, rear-engined Routemaster, FRM1.

It was in 1948 that I moved from Winterbourne Primary to Whitgift Middle School and met Barry who lived at Wallington, which was not only the terminus of the 234/234A but also not too far from Kingston, where, on an expedition organised by Barry, I discovered that single-deckers were not just encountered but far outnumbered buses with stairs. This was partly because many of Kingston's routes served the Surrey countryside — not exactly a sparsely populated wilderness, more an area where there was probably a greater proportion of households possessing cars (and also the means to acquire rationed petrol) than in most other parts of the kingdom — and also passed over insubstantial bridges or under low ones. Here more ageing LTs — and Ts, these being four-wheel AEC Regals of similar vintage — predominated, although there were also some postwar buses in the shape of Weymann-bodied Ts and TDs. The TDs were Leyland PS1 Tigers, some with Weymann bodywork identical to that fitted to the Ts, others with Mann Egerton bodies.

The Weymann bodies were of pure provincial design with sliding-vent windows, a most unusual feature for London, but the Mann Egerton bodies had a distinctly Chiswick air about them. Mann Egerton had never built bodies for London buses before, although it had refurbished many immediately after the war. A number of Ts and LTs were similarly dealt with, in this case by Marshall of Cambridge. The rebuilt Ts and LTs had much simplified panelling and a livery of red all over, save for a narrow cream line below the windows. Instead of grab handles on the backs of the seats the LTs had poles extending to the roof, which no doubt added stability to the structure, and internally were generally smartened up in an effort to persuade passengers that they were actually second cousins of the RT family which was then entering service in vast numbers. It wasn't a bad try.

The arrival of the RF class from 1951 quickly wiped out the prewar single-deckers. Remarkably T31, dating from the last day of 1929, remained in passenger service until July 1952, but even then London Transport was loath to part with it, and it served as a trainer until June 1956. It was then based

*Left:* A former Green Line 10T10 coach of London Transport, relegated to staff transport and photographed on the forecourt of Reigate garage in 1955.

*Above:* **Single-deckers outnumber double-deckers in London Transport's Kingston bus station in 1949. Centre-stage is an LT-class AEC Renown dating from 1931.**

at Norbiton, which had been opened in 1952 just down the road from Kingston, which was of limited capacity and was also serving as a bus station, and therefore bursting at the seams. By this date the private preservation movement was just beginning, and three young men whose names would become renowned — Ken Blacker, Prince Marshall and Michael Dryhurst — plus others managed to raise £45 to buy T31, which is why it is now one of the stars of the London Bus Preservation Trust's collection, beautifully restored to the condition in which it entered service with London General more than 80 years ago.

When new T31 had a cut-away rear entrance, just like contemporary double-deckers but a fairly unusual feature for a single-decker. All the Ts were soon being rebuilt with a forward entrance, and the only similar vehicle I can recall ever seeing is a

preserved Exeter Corporation TS8 Tiger of 1938, with a Cravens 32-seat body. Of course, there's no reason why single-deckers shouldn't be so designed; we're talking about an era where there was always a conductor, so from that point of view it didn't matter whether the entrance was in the front, the middle or the rear. Edinburgh had some, but all had gone by the time of my first visit to that most beautiful of cities, in 1960.

My next acquaintance with single-deckers was in Shropshire, where my mum's relations lived in the northern reaches of the vast Midland Red territory.

*Right:* **A preserved London Transport TD-class Leyland Tiger PS1 with Mann Egerton body, participating in the 1975 HCVC London–Brighton run.**

*Left:* The limited space provided for the driver's cab on a Midland Red SON is clearly seen on this bus heading through Dogpole on its way to Shrewsbury town centre in 1955. The bus was new in 1937.

I had never seen anything like the buses which climbed Shrewsbury's hilly streets and ventured out into the high-hedged lanes of north Shropshire, passing the fields where Uncle Frank kept the cows belonging to Mr Crowe on the Hardwick estate of the Bibby family, who had made their fortune in the Liverpool-based shipping company of that name. It was not until we visited another aunt and uncle in Stafford that I realised the Midland Red fleet was not made up entirely of single-deckers, but they certainly had a monopoly around Shrewsbury. They had silver roofs (even though this was wartime), minimal mudguards and were high off the ground, and defining them as half cabs was stretching things more than somewhat, for the cabs were tiny and when viewed front-on appeared to take up something less than a third of the available space. The space allocated to the engine was similarly

*Below:* **Midland Red pioneered the widespread use of underfloor-engined buses. The S6 on the left was new in 1946, the S12 alongside in 1950. They are seen in Shrewsbury garage in 1956.**

miserly, yet this was clearly powerful enough to haul 38 seated passengers — six more than most single-deckers of the period — and several more standing.

My recollections of actually travelling on a Midland Red single-decker at that time are a bit hazy, for we normally went into Shrewsbury by train, but I do recall once waiting at the roadside for one and it sailing past, the conductor indicating that he was already full to capacity. At first glance a prewar IM, ON, CON, DON or SON appeared to be door-less, as in London, but this was not so, for at the top of the two steps leading to the interior was a swing door under the control of the conductor.

Later I travelled on Midland Red single-deckers of the late 1940s and early 1950s; the contrast could hardly have been more extreme. Whilst the SON was still in production in the late 1930s the company was experimenting with a revolutionary rear-engined layout. Despite the advent of war these experiments continued, the engine position changing from rear to underfloor, within the wheelbase, and in 1946 the first of 100 S6 40-seat buses went into production. These were followed by the 8ft-wide S8s, and later both types were

*Right:* A Maidstone & District Strachans-bodied Bristol L5G of 1941, outside London's Victoria Coach Station in 1954.

lengthened to become 44-seaters. Midland Red had quite simply beaten the big boys, Leyland and AEC, Dennis, Guy and Daimler, and I often think that insufficient credit is given to the company for this quite extraordinary achievement.

Plenty of double-deck bodies were built during World War 2 and fitted to a variety of chassis, old and new, but practically all wartime single-deckers were Bedford OWB normal-control 30-seaters. They could be seen the length and breadth of Britain but were not much use to the hard-pressed major operators and were mostly to be found performing rural duties in the ownership of small, local firms. Whenever we visited Wem, which was on the extreme north-westerly fringe of Midland Red territory, on market day there was always at least one grey-painted normal-control OWB to be seen, its driver collecting the fares from the passengers as they boarded, laden down with the finest sausages and pork pies ever, before setting off for the Welsh Marches.

The only normal-length, half-cab wartime body I ever came across was that fitted to a Maidstone & District Bristol L5G of 1941 vintage. We met in one of the squares close to Victoria Coach Station, where it was laying over, having been pressed into long-distance service from the Medway Towns. It had the high, prewar-style radiator and whilst its Strachans body was reasonably curvaceous it was of typically skimpy wartime appointment within, and its passengers must have thought themselves hard done by in comparison with the fine Harrington- and Beadle-bodied coaches amongst which it was parked.

Contrasting with the situation at Midland Red, the immediate postwar single-deckers of many companies — Ribble, East Kent and Maidstone & District immediately spring to mind — were scarcely distinguishable from their late-prewar predecessors, not least because these latter were sometimes fitted with postwar bodies. Ribble mounted postwar Burlingham bodies on prewar Leyland Tiger TS7 chassis, and East Kent put new Park Royal bodies on a number of its 1936/7-vintage Dennis Lancets, whilst many prewar Maidstone & District Tigers and AEC Regal coaches received bodywork of pure prewar design post 1945. All these rapidly became even more antiquated with the universal adoption in the early 1950s of the underfloor engine layout. Some soldiered on, lasting in a few cases into the 1960s. East Kent glued — well, that's how it looked — full fronts onto some of its Lancets and fooled no-one. In the early 1950s both East Kent and Maidstone & District placed into service a large number of Beadle semi-chassisless coaches with prewar components, which vehicles were rendered obsolete almost instantaneously by their underfloor-engined successors, the Maidstone examples being rapidly demoted to buses.

We have noted that the normal-control bus was still alive and kicking during the World War 2 years, in the shape of the OWB. Vastly better appointed was the classic Duple-bodied Bedford OB, production of which had just begun when the war broke out and which had then to be suspended in favour of the much more basic OWB. With the war over the OB soon became the most popular coach in the UK, its production outstripping that of all its rivals. It also served as a bus, and came the favoured choice of countless rural operators, fulfilling their every need, taking children to school, older members of the family to town, and groups to the seaside and London at weekends. So popular and so long-lived was it that if a film or TV company today wants 'an old-fashioned bus' it invariably plumps for a preserved Bedford/Duple OB, continuing a long tradition which began when it was still

relatively new, as in the 1953 film *The Titfield Thunderbolt*, in which, in the charge of actor Sid James, an OB plays the villain to the Liverpool & Manchester Railway locomotive Lion, which takes the part of the 'Titfield Thunderbolt' itself.

The OB was not the only normal-control chassis in production in the immediate postwar years, and a surprising number of prewar normal-control vehicles survived well into the 1950s. On a visit to the Isle of Wight in May 1955 I came across a prewar Southern Vectis Dennis Ace parked beside Newport garage. With its pronounced snout and quite impressive turn of speed it was no wonder the little Ace was nicknamed the 'Flying Pig.' The Ace was a popular choice with many companies — East Kent had some, as did Maidstone & District. After the war the latter converted four of them to open-toppers and used them around Hastings

*Above:* A Bedford OB with Duple Vista body is seen in the company of a London Transport 'E1' tram in Wandsworth at the end of the 1940s. The OB was an extremely popular model with coach operators large and small.

and elsewhere. The Ace's postwar successor, the Falcon, was bought by Maidstone & District, East Kent and, of course, Aldershot & District, which, with a number of routes passing the Dennis factory at Guildford, was, not surprisingly, that manufacturer's best customer.

The most popular prewar forward-control chassis was the Leyland Cub. Southdown, Ribble, East Kent, Crosville and London Transport were just five of the companies which bought it. The Southdown and London Transport examples

*Left:* Many Bedford OBs survive in preservation. This Duple-bodied coach was new to Western National in 1949 and is seen in Winchester 60 years later in the livery of Mervyns Coaches, of Dummer. It is participating in the annual January running day organised by the Friends of King Alfred Buses.

I knew well. I used to come across the London Transport version working out of Chelsham garage on the 464 and 465 routes. The latter terminated at Holland, a destination which threw me not a little until I looked it up in one of those excellent area timetables which London Transport published, initially at a cost of two old pence, and discovered that the said Holland was a hamlet south of Oxted. When the time came to withdraw the Cubs in 1953 their replacements were not, as might have been expected, shortened versions of an AEC or Leyland underfloor engined bus but normal-control Guys. There were 84 of these GS-class buses. To quote the 1954 edition of the Ian Allan ABC of London Transport, 'The bodywork — with electrically operated folding door — is designed to L.T.E. requirements but in certain features is unmistakeably E.C.W.' with their 'front end a standard Briggs pressing as used on Fordson Thames trucks'. They were handsome little vehicles, lasting long into the underfloor-engined era. They are still a familiar sight, for the quite remarkable total of 26 has been preserved.

The open-top single-decker was a bit of a rarity but could sometimes be found by the seaside. The Maidstone & District Aces lasted until 1958, eventually being withdrawn at the grand old age of 24. They were succeeded by three 1946/7 Beadle-bodied Regal buses similarly converted in 1957/8. Two of these were even longer-lived than the Aces, serving 36 years with the company, until 1983, and

continuing thereafter with the new Hastings & District company. All three have been preserved.

Southport Corporation went in for the open-top single-decker in a big way. I once hired one of its open-top Burlingham-bodied PS2 Tigers, ex Ribble, to publicise an art-school summer dance. Far and away the most unusual open-top single-deckers ever to operate within these shores must surely be the ex-Army Bedford lorries which Southport Corporation acquired and converted to take passengers along the beach. The sea at low tide disappeared — and still does — way beyond the end of the pier, despite this itself being long enough to warrant a tramway, leaving enough sand to accommodate not just a bus route and most of the population of Merseyside but also an airstrip, from which it was possible to take pleasure flights out across the Ribble estuary and over Blackpool Tower. And, in the 1920s, the world land-speed record was attempted there; but not by a Corporation bus.

# A shot in the dark

**Digital imaging has the potential to revolutionise night-time photography. John Robinson explores the possibilities.**

*All photographs by the author*

Although I have been taking night photographs of buses and other transport subjects since 1977, continuing advances in digital camera technology have opened up possibilities for after-dark photography that were completely unthinkable with traditional film cameras.

One of these is the ability to use high ISO (sensitivity) settings in digital without the same level of 'grain' (called 'noise' in digital photography) that would be apparent using film at an equivalent speed. In addition, ISO settings on digital cameras can be changed from one exposure to the next, as required; with film you were normally committed until the roll was finished unless you changed rolls mid-stream or used a camera with interchangeable film backs.

The camera used for all the pictures in this feature was a Nikon D700, which has a top ISO

setting of 25,600, although both Nikon and Canon now have professional cameras in their ranges with maximum ISO settings of 102,400 which can take pictures in virtual darkness! In the future even higher maximum ISO settings are likely to be offered by camera manufacturers.

Coupled with high-quality 'fast' (i.e. having a large maximum aperture) prime lenses such as the Nikon 50mm f1.4, which was used for all of these photographs, the opportunity to photograph moving buses in reasonably well illuminated locations has presented itself.

This frees up the need to use a tripod, which is generally required for after-dark photography using film, so allows photography at locations other than just those where buses would be stationery such as bus stations, traffic lights and depots. Also there are a lot of locations where it simply wouldn't be practical to use a tripod because of the obstruction, and possible danger, it would cause to pedestrians or traffic, not to mention the photographer!

All these pictures were shot in RAW, which I now use exclusively; shooting in this mode, rather than JPEG, produces larger image files due to the increased detail recorded. Consequently there is far more latitude for 'processing' RAW files than JPEGs.

These RAW files have been processed in Nikon Capture NX2 software. Amongst a host of features, this allows adjustments to be made to contrast and brightness, along with the correction of any colour casts caused by the artificial lighting present

*Left:* **National Express West Midlands' Walsall garage bade farewell to its final MCW Metrobuses on 28 November 2009, 2887 (C887 FON), allocated to Walsall throughout its life, operating the town's very last scheduled Metrobus service, a short working of the 341 Willenhall route to the delightfully named New Invention. It is seen loading in Walsall's St Pauls Street bus station before departing on this historic journey. West Midlands' last Metrobuses ran from Acocks Green garage in Birmingham, on 24 July 2010.**

at night. The resulting, improved images are then saved in JPEG format, whilst the original RAW image file always remains unchanged, akin to a negative in film terminology.

Another benefit of digital is that a test shot can be taken at the chosen location to ensure the exposure is correct before taking the main shot. Whilst it is always best to get the exposure correct at the time of taking the picture, checking the image and histogram on the camera's monitor, shooting images in RAW allows some latitude with exposure. Potentially compensation can be applied in the software equivalent to +/- two stops to correct any under- or over-exposure. Localised lightening and darkening of selected parts of the image can also be undertaken. Shadow detail, for example around the wheel arches or beneath the bus, or in the foreground or background, may not be visible in the unconverted RAW file but once the software is applied it can be brought out. However, it is important for these changes to be subtle if the finished image is to look realistic and not 'overdone'.

Although it is always good practice to have a filter over the lens (UV or similar) for protection, at night bright light sources, such as vehicle headlights

or street lights, can be reflected by the filter onto the camera's image sensor causing their ghostly image to appear in the picture. I have found that removing the filter overcomes this problem; however, it is vital that extra care is taken with the unprotected lens to avoid any damage.

The selection of photographs which follow were taken at ISO settings ranging from 800 to 1,600 and apertures between F1.4 and F4. When the lens is fully open (f1.4) or thereabouts the depth of field

*Above:* **Pictured in Pound Tree Road, Southampton in November 2010 while operating service 5 to Lordshill is a First Wright-bodied Volvo B10BLE new in 1998.**

is relatively shallow, especially with a full-frame camera like the D700. This means that features in the foreground and background will be rendered in slightly softer focus than the main subject, the bus, which is what the autofocus locked onto.

With the faster shutter speeds possible with digital in night photography any moving people appearing in the picture are less of a problem as they can now be rendered sharp, rather than as ghostly blurs, which was the case with the longer exposures required when using film. If they are in the right position within the overall composition, the inclusion of people can bring a bus photograph to life rather than it simply being a pure technical 'record' shot. Night shots also have the advantage that passengers are generally well illuminated, which can reveal some interesting off-guard moments!

These faster shutter speeds also overcome the problem of the movement of stationary buses in the

*Left:* **Working the X5 service from Cambridge to Oxford, a Stagecoach United Counties Plaxton Panther-bodied Volvo B9R pulls away from its stop in St Neots Market Square in December 2010. The X5 is now operated by a dedicated fleet of 17 such coaches, based at Bedford depot.**

act of 'kneeling' at bus stops, which, with the longer exposure times necessary with film, causes them to be rendered less than sharp.

Destination displays can be problematical at night, particularly those comprising LEDs (light-emitting diodes), as these are generally much brighter than the rest of the bus so tend to be over-exposed when the image is shot. The extent of over-exposure will vary depending on the general level of light illuminating the bus; if it is relatively high the exposure will be shorter so the 'bleaching out' of the destination is not as pronounced, whereas a longer exposure in darker conditions will accentuate the problem. To some extent the problem can be resolved at the processing stage, using software to darken or lighten this part of the image.

*Right:* **The varied Centrebus fleet includes this Optare Olympus-bodied Scania N230UD, seen leaving St Margaret's bus station, Leicester, in January 2011.**

*Below:* **A yellow-liveried Scania CN94UB OmniCity of Nottingham City Transport operating a park-and-ride service in Upper Parliament Street in January 2011.**

Flip-dot destination displays, made up of hundreds of dots covered in a reflective surface material illuminated by a strip of LEDs mounted — out of sight — at the bottom of the housing, tend to be less problematical in night photography, as does the traditional roller blind.

Both LED and flip-dot destinations may be scrolling at the point a photograph is taken, whether day or night, which means the display may be 'broken up' if caught at the moment it is changing or — even less welcome — show a completely blank screen. I usually take three or four pictures in rapid succession using the motor drive, to increase the chances of at least one image showing the full display.

*Left:* Nottingham City Transport acquired Pathfinder (Newark) in 1997 and retains the fleetname for its 100 service from Nottingham to Southwell. Here an Optare Versa, one of five so branded, turns into King Street, its city terminus, from Upper Parliament Street in January 2011.

*Below:* A busy scene in Humberstone Gate, Leicester, in January 2011, with three First Volvos — two Wright-bodied B7Ls passing a B7TL with Alexander ALX400 bodywork.

Some of the most attractive night shots can be obtained whilst there are still traces of natural colour in the sky, rather than it being completely black, which tends to occur within the 30 minutes after sunset and the 30 minutes before sunrise. This may also allow slightly shorter exposures, thus alleviating the problem with LED destinations.

Night photography has suddenly become a lot easier than it used to be; it's just a pity that the current digital camera technology didn't exist in much earlier times, when, to me (and no doubt many other readers), the British bus scene was a lot more varied and interesting.

*Left:* Passing beneath Coventry's Whittle Arch in December 2010 is a National Express Coventry TransBus-bodied Volvo B7TL. The arch was constructed to commemorate Sir Frank Whittle, inventor of the jet engine, who was born in the city.

*Below:* Picking up at St Margaret's bus station, Leicester, on National Express service 310 from Birmingham to Bradford is a Caetano-bodied Volvo B9R, one of five delivered in 2010 to Excelsior of Bournemouth.

# Tired of life?

**Robert E. Jowitt**, in usual irrelevant or irreverent vein, discourses on more than six decades of acquaintanceship with the buses of the Metropolis, with a few foreign comparisons and a useful commentary on statues and postcards.

*All photographs by the author*

'When a man is tired of London,' quoth Samuel Johnson (is he related to London's latest Johnson, one wonders) in one of many letters to his friend Boswell, on 22 September 1777, 'he is tired of life…'

I think I agree with him, though London is not my favourite capital city. In truth (and though be it banal and obvious to say so) while part of it is known as 'the City', much of it is a series of different districts disparate in character, architecture and inhabitants. Some people regard the hub of its centre as the Houses of Parliament and Westminster Abbey, some as the Bank or the Tower, others as Buckingham Palace, others again, perhaps mostly foreigners, as Trafalgar Square or Piccadilly Circus. The main common linking feature between these many diverse spots is the London omnibus, scarlet-painted etc as rendered famous in song by Flanders and Swann. This is possibly one of the best songs about London; personally I do not rate 'Maybe it's because I'm a Londoner' very highly.

Mind you, 'Sous les ponts de Paris' and 'I love Paris in the springtime' are not the most inspiring of ditties either. Paris, however, with its Haussmann boulevards, boasts an architectural unity and thus a grandeur lacking in London, unless you count the solid Victorian bourgeois terrace styles, in varying degrees of respectability, from Bloomsbury to Kensington and Chelsea. But Paris has buses which have gradually or even rapidly diminished in charm since the cessation four decades ago of the 60-year career of the famous open-platforms, so that even if they are still a uniting factor from arrondissement to arrondissement they are nowadays an insipid one — and not in the true green-and-cream as applied from 1910 to 1970. I guess the statue of Henri IV on the Pont Neuf, if he still looks as if he is waving buses encouragingly onwards, seems a bit half-hearted about these dismal bathroom-suite tints. How right was Red Ken to insist that red London buses should remain red, whate'er else might betide!

The first time I ever encountered the buses of London, that which impressed me most was the fact that they had 'eyes'. This was in the latter half of the 1940s, when as a child I was taken by my parents to the Science Museum … where, so it has been told me, I danced with delight at the model locomotives in glass cases; you could push a button and watch the motion functioning. I dare say they may these days be in the infamous store. We rode on a bus, I do recall, and for all I know it may have been an LT. I like to imagine it was. I am sure, anyway, that it had eyes. The eyes were, of course, the celebrated advertisements for Picture Post, a remarkably accurate reproduction of a human eye on either side of the front destination display, certainly one of the most successful bus posters ever. Dare I suggest 'eye-catching'?

We saw trams too, but for some reason my father failed to take me on them, though at that date we would have been able to thread the Kingsway Subway. What a pity! Despite this lapse he maintained a useful notion, this being that should you chance to be bored in London, even if not tired of life, you could cure the boredom by boarding the first bus to appear, bidding the conductor 'Terminus, please,' and be wafted whither the wind willed … or rather the route. I have tried it, with some pleasure, more than once. It may be feasible in this new century, though I cannot guarantee it, to catch a glimpse of statues of Churchill, Lloyd George, Nelson, 'Bomber' Harris and Wellington all from one bus, but perchance 'a damned close-run thing!', not possible in my father's time because some of those subjects were still alive …

Albeit that my first ride may not have been on an LT, the LT was to me for a long time the classic London bus. I had a fine book entitled *Overground*, with details of London buses, and also numerous picture postcards, and the LT with its splendid three axles and various styles of front and stairs allured me, though probably after that initial visit I never saw one in service again.

*Right:* **An RTL bound for Hammersmith Broadway passes a trolleybus heading for Harlesden in this 1960 view. The trolleybus is a 70-seat Leyland of 1939.**

Verily, throughout the 1950s my journeys through London, such as they were, were probably in taxicabs, to go from Waterloo to King's Cross or wherever it might be for journeys onwards. 'This is a proper old London taxi,' my father would say. A square one, like the Triang Minic toy I cherished, but they too were becoming rare.

My attention was brought back seriously to London Transport by the impending scrapping of the trolleybuses, a form of traction to which I had already become considerably devoted. You could never be tired of life while you travelled around the peripheries of London in what was boasted to be the largest trolleybus system in the world (possibly bar Moscow, but who knew anything about that, save only that the Russians had launched the Sputnik — and I still have postage stamps to prove it).

The London trolleybuses, below an incredible spider's web of complex overhead wiring, exhibited the truth of the diversity of outer London just as much as RTs could visit manifold facets of

the more central areas. Out here you had old towns swamped and overtaken by the spawning growth of metropolitan housing, huge rashes of Edwardian or between-the-wars architectural development or dreadfulness. I spent many happy hours exploring these profundities, in the intervals of attending GCEs at the University of London or some such place, and utterly deplored the incoming Routemasters with their nasty new 200-series route numbers replacing the old 600s of the trolleys. What I did not discover, until about 35 years too late, was that on the routes between North Finchley and Cricklewood I had missed a fantastic statue of a naked lady raising a sword heavenwards.

But yes, I did achieve an A level in French, which was to stand me in good stead in subsequent adventures regarding my acquisition of withdrawn Paris buses, to whose native city, after exploration of such European capitals as Brussels and Den Haag, I finally succumbed.

I have made mention of Paris herein already, so will not mention it again. As for Den Haag, it

*Right:* **Three trolleybuses — that's a 1938 AEC 664T nearest the camera — and an RT congregate at Aldwych.**

*Right:* Certain sections of London's trolleybus routes were equipped, in the style of some Continental tramways, with bow-string overhead arms. Two trolleybuses pass on route 697, which ran between Chingford Mount and the Docks.

*Left:* Four trolleybuses at the Docks in 1960, accompanied by cyclists.

*Right:* An RTL and a Routemaster on layover at The Eagle, Portobello Road, in 1965.

included in that era various magnificent inter-urban trams, soon wantonly to die. The place now has quite decent modern trams, and a statue — fairly recent, I think — which though basically a crude block of stone in the shape of a stocky lady, offers a fine vision of the fighting spirit of Queen Wilhelmina.

Brussels had networks of trams on two gauges, often prettily mixed, but it has seemed to me in retrospect to be but a poor imitation of Paris — and what more might be expected of a city whose best-known symbol, may it be argued, is a small statue of a small boy relieving himself? Brussels' other claim to fame might be the Atomium, predating the Sputnik by a couple of years but looking like a cluster of Sputniks sewn together. I probably possess a postage stamp of that too. It was served by a respectable tram route, solidarity in an age of modernity. Brussels has now buried its metre-gauge trams in scrapyards and many of the standard-gauge cars in dark subways, but in the mostly tram-less streets there remain glorious examples of art nouveau architecture.

My wanderings took me also, via another (then) capital, Bonn, 'a small town in Germany', with boring trams and some pleasantly elderly trolleybuses, to Vienna, of not un-Parisian architectural splendour but with red-and-white trams instead of green-and-cream buses. Hundreds of them, and some as old as or even older than Parisian buses. It boasts also a very fine statue of Johann Strauss. I confess I cannot recall if really

I have ever seen this, but am well familiar with it from the covers of many gramophone records, the Blue Danube and so on, though in truth I prefer the more subtle waltzes of Josef Strauss, and the Danube is not blue, rather murky grey — and out in a somewhat dingy side of Vienna at that, not grandly through the centre like the Seine. Even, in

*Right:* A 1967 view of a Routemaster heading towards Parliament Square.

*Left:* A remarkably traffic-free view of Big Ben, with an RT and, in the background, an XA-class Atlantean. The cars are both Fords — an Anglia and a Prefect.

un-amenable part of the scene I learned to accept the RM. I had to admit it looked fairly traditional.

My wife at that time had eyesight problems, and for her the only answer was a clinic somewhere off Oxford Street. I had a jolly time, during her consultations, with RTs and RMs in the vicinity, after which we might stray down Kings Road, Chelsea, with a constant background of more RMs and RTs and a foreground of Mary Quant miniskirts.

We also briefly explored another European capital — stolid Bern, which, while served by stolid trams and trolleybuses, was chiefly notable for a clock-tower, a pit housing real live bears, and a horrid statue of a giant devouring children. Even the worst of London cannot offer anything so grotesque!

Apart from Luxembourg and Lisbon, with which fair cities I have dealt liberally in earlier editions of this work and on which I shall therefore eschew further comment (and should I throw in Liechtenstein, through which I once briefly passed and admired a Swiss-type post-bus?) I feel I should utter, after the western extremity of Lisbon, some words on other far-west capitals, such as Cardiff, which, one time or another, on social or business grounds, I have visited both in trolleybus days and later; but here again I have uttered words on it before in *Buses Yearbook*, if briefly, so will skip more now, especially as, though I suppose it must contain a statue of the Marquis of Bute, I doubt I

comparison, the Thames does pretty well.

The Thames Embankment reveals a sporting statue of Boadicea. Trams which passed her were long defunct. Trolleybuses never passed her and by the early 1960s passed nowhere in London at all. The RM was a fait accompli, and, as one gradually learns to accept new buses as on the whole a not

*Left:* Oxford Street, near Marble Arch, in 1972. Routemasters rule.

*Right:* **As late as 1998 Routemasters still outnumber more modern types in Oxford Street.**

have seen this. I am bound also to skip two other capitals, this time because they are unknown to me, even though Belfast once had a huge trolleybus network and Dublin vast throngs of green buses, as picture postcards indicate, and presently has a new tramway and a sexy statue of Molly Malone. I should inspect it; I have sung of her often enough. I could inspect green pillar boxes at the same time.

If I move on to the last but not least of capitals in the British Isles I can recall my most recent exploration, in the late 1990s, of Edinburgh, but here again my admiration for the huge herds of buses of the Athens of the North has been expressed in *Buses Yearbook*, so we will leave it, passing perhaps en route by a statue of some brave hussar on Princes Street, on whose shako pigeons delight in perching, and the much-loved image of the much-loved dog Greyfriars Bobby.

If statues are renowned in Rome and Madrid, these are capitals beyond my ken (ha ha!). Likewise the more newly accessible ones (formerly red, ha ha again!) such as Prague and Warsaw, if not quite a closed book — for I possess plenty of books devoted to them — are mere armchair joys. I will adhere forthwith to the capital of the Empire on which the sun never sets. Or does it?

I must admit that after the trolleybuses were dead I never, for decades, attacked London with the specific intention of studying buses, if never tiring of RTs and RMs; they were simply there, the regular

picture-postcard backdrop brought to life … along with a sprinkling of rather jolly little creatures known as Red Arrows (a name more

*Right:* **An Arriva Mercedes-Benz Citaro crosses London Bridge, with the 'Gherkin' prominent on the skyline.**

famous, perhaps, in aviation). These were a small group fitted for flat fares with turnstiles, part of a larger collection of more normal single-deckers — eventually, over six years from 1966, more than 1,000 AEC Swifts. It has been stated — though pundits tend to swear erroneous beliefs — that they were unpopular in operation and mechanically seedy.

I was sorry, of course, when it became time for the RTs to start disappearing, and I could hardly admire various OMO boxes, most notorious among them the DMSs, which were brought in to replace them. Some of the various boxes were, apparently, rapidly deemed unsuitable for a city well versed in the ways of the open-rear platform, and while RMs and RMLs thrived newer vehicles turned up second-hand all over the country. In the 1980s, when I was resident in Winchester, we had a batch of former DMSs working for Hampshire Bus from Southampton (with the centre exit removed) and some of those merry little Swifts coming in on rural services operated by Hants & Sussex (a name familiar in the Winchester area in the 1950s, thereafter long dormant, but revived for a new foray from Bishops Waltham), albeit still not noted for their mechanical reliability, I seem to recall. As I have been discussing capital cities I may here observe that Winchester was, centuries ago, the capital of all England! King Alfred, apart from burning cakes, is famed for giving his name, 1,000 years after his death, to a renowned bus company, whose vehicles bore on their sides a likeness of his statue by Hamo Thornycroft.

Naturally, despite antipathy towards some of the boxes and their failures and unsuitability, boxes became more and more the norm, while RMs were becoming rarer birds. I was struck, after an absence of several years, when I walked down Oxford Street in 1998, by how many boxes there were; however, rightly believing that RMs and RMLs, while still abundant, would soon not be so, I lavished on these far more photographic attention than on the boxes — in retrospect perhaps a pity, for the contemporary generation would be despatched as speedily as the ancient jewels. What struck me more was how many mobile phones there were. By now resident in rural Herefordshire, I was scarcely aware of the existence of such devices, but here every second or third dolly-bird (though I suspect the term was by now archaic) was yakking into one. We were truly entering a new era.

Ironically this new dawn rendered the dying RM more popular than ever before, along the lines, I suppose, that you cherish your everyday treasures only when you are about to be robbed of them. It is worth remarking, even if a well-known fact, that many RMs, after a far longer London life than newer vehicles, enjoyed a new second-hand adventure in regular service in other towns and cities, notably Southampton, Reading, Blackpool and Glasgow. Meanwhile, back in London, postcards of RMs abounded on souvenir stalls, many being cut-out silhouettes, usually lopping mirrors and other excrescences and sometimes even bits of bodywork to produce hideously distorted likenesses. Prices varied from reasonable, area by area, to gross profiteering. Even today, when surviving RMs represent little more than a ghostly tourist trap, the cards are still on sale. (I believe you can buy red pillar boxes and red telephone boxes in the same fashion, equally extortionate. I wonder if they sell green silhouette pillar-boxes in Dublin.)

*Left:* In 2010 the Routemasters have gone, but the Oxford Street lamp standards are still the same. A Transdev Scania approaches.

This new era, besides, had abandoned the title 'LONDON TRANSPORT' on the buses' flanks, and we were faced with strange notions, Arriva and the like — I knew not (and still know not) what! Heaven be praised, if there was a dash of white or blue here and there along with the new names, the main colour, as I have stated above, remained red.

More was to follow. Shall I say 'worse'? In the first years of the new century I was dragged around the streets of London by my new Dutch South African girlfriend, given to sightseeing, to find them disfigured by bendybuses. This is not actually a term I care to use; 'articulateds' is quite good enough for me. As my regular readers will know, I have, in general, a long-standing fondness for this type of bus … on the Continent. In the streets of London it appeared utterly out of place. It gained moreover a reputation for being liable to burst into flames at any moment, though the number of times this catastrophe occurred can probably be counted on the fingers of one or two hands. It also became notorious as easy prey for fare-dodgers. At all events the luckless creature, like the DMS before it, was condemned — probably unfairly — to early ousting, though at the time I am writing not a few are yet snaking around, lasting longer than the Dutch South African lady, who returned to her native shores, or the Oud Transvaal; sic transit gloria mundi. Because of my predilection for the type in general, even if disgusted at its presence on British highways (the articulated, I mean), I set out,

for once in a while, to spend time in its pursuit. I will not go so far as to say I went to London for this sole purpose, but I so planned my journeys — one of them was to Cambridge, if anybody cares — to allow myself adequate time in the Metropolis for the chase of aliens.

In this intention there were other forces at play. If you have read this article with due attention you will have noticed mention made, more than once, of Oxford Street. Now lately Oxford Street seems to have become increasingly served by buses, other transport being, bar taxis, largely banned — in my view quite rightly so. It is said to see pass some 300 buses an hour. To me there has always been a certain splendour about buses en masse. In a similar vein, even six pigeons perched on a telegraph wire look better than one solitary specimen… and Oxford Street is a very paradise in this respect (the buses, not the abundant pigeons). Some spoilsports, however, object to this intensive progress. It has been described — I recall not by whom; perhaps even by Red Ken, perhaps by Blue Boris, perhaps by opponents of either or both of them — as 'a mobile wall of shivering red metal' or words to that effect.

As for me, in the fear that the whole business, even if of mere boxes nowadays, might be swept away (though quite what else could be done about the problem is debatable) I again set out deliberately to record the riot, and absolutely made the most of it, loved every minute; are my mathematics correct in estimating it as five buses a minute? And if so who could fail to enjoy it? And I realised full well that, mess though in many ways it be, I was far from tired of London. Or of life!

*Below:* **A Metroline Plaxton-bodied Volvo B7TL in Oxford Street, overseen by a pretty lady promoting … who knows what?**

# Hertfordshire independents

**Mark Bailey** illustrates some of the smaller operators that have provided services in Hertfordshire.

*All photographs by the author*

For many years London Transport was the dominant provider of bus and coach services in the county of Hertfordshire. This changed in 1970, when the green country operations were separated out to form London Country Bus Services. Further fragmentation occurred in 1986, when, in the run-up to privatisation, LCBS was itself split into four, Hertfordshire being served by the North East and North West companies.

Around the same time the deregulation of local bus services gave Hertfordshire County Council the ability to invite operators to tender for contracts, in order to plug gaps in service provision and safeguard vulnerable services. The ensuing 25 years has seen operators come and go and contracts change hands on a regular basis, and today the county's bus scene continues to offer significant variety and interest.

*Right:* **Kingsman Travel began operating Harpenden town services in 1977. Pictured in April 1983 working route HA1 is an ECW-bodied Bristol LHS6L which had been new to London Country. Vehicles wore a distinctive livery of pink and blue and were named after characters in Arthurian legend, this one being Sir Bedivere.**

*Left:* **During the 1970s and 80s Charles Cook operated service CC1 from Biggleswade, in neighbouring Bedfordshire, to Stevenage, via Stotfold and Baldock. Loadings were often sufficient to justify double-deck operation, and several ex-London Transport DMS-class Fleetlines and MD-class Metropolitans were deployed. Pictured at Stevenage's Lister Hospital in April 1984 is a Metropolitan. The service passed to Stagecoach-owned United Counties in 1989 and was renumbered 191.**

*Left:* Sworders of Walkern had a very smart fleet and concentrated primarily on school contracts. Pictured in 1984 are, from the left, an ECW-bodied Bristol LH6L new to London Transport, a Willowbrook-bodied Leyland Leopard new to Trent and a Willowbrook-bodied Bedford YRT new to United Counties.

*Right:* Premier Travel operated two coach services (78 and 79) from its base in Cambridge to Luton, Heathrow and Gatwick airports. The 78 provided a useful link between Royston, Baldock, Letchworth and Hitchin, while the 79 served Stevenage, until the route was altered to take in Stansted Airport instead. Seen in Stevenage in April 1987 is a Plaxton Supreme V-bodied Bedford YNT acquired the previous year with the Youngs of Rampton business. Unusual for a YNT in being built to 12m length, it was one of three Youngs coaches fitted with a centre door for wheelchair access.

*Below:* Coaching firm Sampsons of Hoddesdon moved into bus operation in 1986, when it won a significant number of contracts, including the complete network of local services in Welwyn Garden City and Hatfield. This April 1987 view at Welwyn Garden City bus station features an ex-United Counties ECW-bodied Bristol RELL6G alongside two ex-South Yorkshire PTE ECW-bodied Daimler Fleetlines. Sampsons' bus operations passed to County Bus & Coach in March 1989.

*Right:* Upon deregulation in 1986 Jubilee Coaches was successful in tendering for a number of Stevenage town services and hastily acquired a fleet of second-hand Daimler Fleetlines to work them. Over the next couple of years, however, it purchased around 30 brand-new vehicles, including 19 MCW Metroriders, six Leyland Lynx and three Duple 300-bodied Leyland Tiger buses. Pictured working town service SB7 in December 1988 is a former Leyland Lynx demonstrator. The following month Jubilee's Stevenage operations were acquired by Sovereign.

*Left:* Welwyn Hatfield Line was launched in 1987 with an initial fleet of 11 Optare CityPacers. As well as services covering the two towns, other HCC contracts were won, including Sunday workings on the 340 to Hemel Hempstead. A CityPacer is seen at the Welwyn Garden City QEII Hospital terminus in July 1989.

*Right:* Smiths of Buntingford was a provider of bus services in northern Hertfordshire for around 60 years, although falling passenger numbers saw most services reduced to market-day operation only. Coaches were mostly deployed, but several buses were also used. An unusual and striking bus was this rare Quest B with Locomotors bodywork, used formerly on car-park shuttle work at Heathrow Airport. It is pictured in August 1989 in Stevenage on the Tuesdays, Fridays and Saturdays service 386 from Standon and Buntingford to Hitchin.

*Above:* Chambers of Stevenage was typical of many established coach companies which saw the opportunity presented by deregulation to venture into service-bus operation. Pictured working HCC route 382 from Letchworth to Stevenage in August 1989 is a Leyland Swift with Wadham Stringer Vanguard II bodywork.

*Below:* BTS was formed as Borehamwood Travel Services in 1984. In the late 1980s several HCC contracts were won, including the local town network and the 355 service to St Albans. Regular performers on the 355 were five low-height Alexander-bodied MCW Metrobuses purchased from Kelvin Scottish, among them this example, seen in St Albans in April 1990. BTS was acquired by Blazefield Holdings in 1994 and subsequently renamed London Sovereign.

*Above:* Luton-based coach operator Seamarks obtained its first HCC contracts in 1989, and for this work four impressive DAF SB220s with Optare Delta bodywork were purchased. This one, coincidentally numbered 220 in the Seamarks fleet, is seen loading in Hitchin on service 88 to Luton in April 1990.

*Below:* Green Rover of Watford commenced operations in 1990 and later that year won the HCC contract for operating Green Line service 724 on Sundays. Appropriately this Park Royal-bodied AEC Reliance, one of 90 RP-class semi-coaches new to London Country in 1971/2 for just this sort of work, was the regular performer on the service and is seen in Welwyn Garden City in October 1991 en route from Harlow to Watford.

*Left:* Established coach company Reg's, formerly of Hertford, ventured into bus operation in the late 1980s, picking up several HCC-contracted routes. Among its vehicle purchases were three early Dennis Darts with Duple Dartline bodywork, two of them being former Duple demonstrators. This one had the lowest-numbered Dart chassis, 101, and is pictured in November 1991 leaving Welwyn Garden City for Hertford on service 388.

*Right:* Universitybus was formed in 1992 to transport students to, from and between campuses of the newly created University of Hertfordshire. The services were open to the general public as well, and passenger numbers grew steadily, leading to an expansion of routes and territory covered. The majority of vehicles were bought new, including four American-built Blue Bird Q RE buses, one of which is pictured in August 1997 in Welwyn Garden City on service 634 to Watford.

*Left:* Formed in 1998, Sullivan Buses of South Mimms runs a number of HCC contracted services in the south of the county, including the local network in Borehamwood. Seen in the town in August 2005 is an unusual Caetano Nimbus-bodied Dennis Dart SLF, working the B3 to Well End.

# When Duple was dominant

In the early 1960s Duple's coach-body designs changed with remarkable rapidity. **Geoff Mills** illustrates some examples.

*Left:* The most common style of Duple body at the start of the 1960s was the Super Vega on Bedford SB chassis, typically with 41 seats. This is actually a 1959 coach which had been new to Sampson of Cheshunt, seen in 1976 in operation with Norfolk's of Nayland. It is a Leyland-engined SB8. Note the two-piece windscreen, soon to be replaced by a new three-piece screen. This coach has chrome wheel discs, a popular 1960s accessory.

*Right:* And here's the three-piece screen, launched in 1961, with an updated grille. This is a 1962 SB3 newly delivered to Osborne's of Tollesbury. The Osborne's coach features glazed cove panels. Note the destination display located in the front bumper. Bedfords of this style weighed less than 5 tons unladen.

*Right:* When the same body was fitted to the Thames chassis it was called the Yeoman. Five were delivered to BET's Hebble subsidiary in 1962. This one is seen in Halifax in 1967. The top-sliding side windows were an option; the standard body had wind-down windows.

*Right:* A broadly similar body was available for underfloor-engined chassis and was called the Britannia. This is a 1961 AEC Reliance in the fleet of Essex County Coaches. All the bodies of this style were built in Duple's factory at Hendon.

*Right:* The curvaceous bodies which typified Duple's output at the start of the decade were replaced from 1962 by new models. In 1960 Duple had taken over Burlingham, of Blackpool, and a new Burlingham model under Duple ownership was the short-lived Gannet for front-engined chassis. In 1962 this Bedford with Gannett body joined the fleet of Norfolk Motor Services of Great Yarmouth.

*Left:* Burlingham was renamed Duple (Northern), and this Blackpool-built Duple Firefly can be seen as a development of the Burlingham Gannett, which it replaced in 1963 after just one season's production. The stylish Firefly was built on Bedford, Ford Thames and, as here, Albion Victor VT21L chassis. New to Staniers of Newchapel in 1964, it is seen in the ownership of PMT in 1973.

*Right:* Rare indeed was the Firefly-style body for underfloor-engined chassis — the Dragonfly. Four on 36ft-long AEC Reliance chassis were delivered to the Samuelson New Transport Co of London in 1963. They were 49-seaters. At this time the Samuelson fleet was 100% Duple. Only six Dragonflys were built, the other two being Leyland Leopard demonstrators.

*Left:* Also developed in Blackpool was the Continental, built only as a 36ft coach on Leyland Leopard and AEC Reliance chassis. A 1962 Leopard in the Ribble fleet-one of a batch of six-is seen in Carlisle in 1966. It was a 40-seater, with a rear toilet compartment.

*Above:* The 1964 Continental had a restyled grille, seen here on an AEC Reliance operated by Osborne's of Tollesbury. The grille improved airflow to the radiator, addressing the problem of Reliances' overheating. Telephone numbers were simpler then; Osborne's was Tollesbury 214, displayed above the garage entrance.

*Below:* The Firefly, Dragonfly and Continental were never mainstream models. The real success for Duple came with the 1962 Bella range of bodies. The Bella Vega was offered on Bedford chassis and was a great success. This is a 1963 Bedford SB5 which had been new to Progressive of Cambridge, and was sold in 1965 to Shamrock & Rambler of Bournemouth. An identical body on the Ford Thames chassis was called the Trooper.

*Above:* On the Bedford VAS chassis Duple built a scaled-down version of the new range, the Bella Vista. The Scottish Bus Group took 29 Bella Vistas in 1962, three of them for Alexander (Midland).

*Below:* The largest of the Bella-style bodies on Bedford chassis was the Vega Major, on the 36ft-long twin-steer VAL. This 52-seater was new in 1963 to Reliance Coaches, of Meppershall, Bedfordshire, and is seen when just a few weeks old. Dinky Toys produced a large-scale model of the Vega Major.

*Above:* On underfloor-engined chassis the equivalent of the Bella models was the Commodore, initially with a similar grille and the same sloping window pillar towards the rear. The range was subsequently refined and by 1965 was branded Commander. This body had a new grille and had lost its sloping pillar, as seen on this Leyland Leopard PSU3/3RT operated by Samuelsons.

*Below:* With the Viceroy, launched at the 1966 Commercial Motor Show, Duple began to standardise body styles for lightweight and heavyweight chassis. Trent took six Viceroys on Bedford VAM5 chassis in 1967. One leaves Nottingham for Skegness when new. The grille was carried over from the Commander, but the rest of the body was new.

*Above:* The Viceroy 36 on the Bedford VAL was not only longer but lower too. Four were delivered in 1967 to Wilts & Dorset in 1967 – unusual purchases for a Tilling-group company. This one is seen in Hants & Dorset ownership four years later, in London's Victoria Coach Station.

*Below:* The Commander developed into a crisp and attractive design, as demonstrated by this 36ft Commander III on a Leopard PSU3/3R chassis, one of two delivered in 1968 to Prince of Wales Coaches, of Ampthill, Bedfordshire. Its styling presaged forthcoming changes to the Viceroy range, which later in 1968 would adopt this design of grille, along with other updates.